for

all the dedicated teachers
who spend endless hours on the job
because they care about their kids
and hope to make a difference in their lives

Contents

Introduction

It's the start of another school year. As I look at the faces of the new students in front of me, I wonder about the unique talents of each child and how I can use that talent to motivate and help them learn. I believe that their wide-ranging abilities and diverse backgrounds enhance their creative thinking and influence achievement. I try to integrate lessons throughout the year that will utilize these talents to strengthen their skills as readers, writers, speakers, and listeners.

These lessons are ones that I've used successfully as a drama specialist and a classroom teacher in the intermediate and middle grades. They incorporate a variety of hands-on activities: games, pantomime, tableau, choral reading, improvisation, Readers Theatre, story enactment, writing in role, debating, interviewing, and performance projects. Working with students of diverse abilities and styles over many years, I have found that these strategies are effective teaching tools that can be powerful additions to a language arts program.

Some of the strategies may already be familiar to teachers. Read-aloud books, choral reading, Readers Theatre, and game playing are popular and frequently used in today's classrooms. But other strategies (pantomime, tableau, improvisation, and enactments, for example) may be less familiar, and teachers might lack the confidence to create and facilitate a lesson that is built around them. I often hear comments such as the following during my teacher workshop presentations: "My kids would love that activity, but I'm not sure I know how to organize and run a lesson like that." Remembering these words, I decided to write this book in lesson format. Each lesson has a specific focus, step-by-step directions for the learning activity, and helpful hints in the "Teacher-to-Teacher" section based on my experience with the lesson.

How to Select Lessons from This Book

All the lessons presented here integrate the essential skills in reading, writing, speaking, or listening. For this reason, they do not take time away from the curriculum but support all strands of language arts.

I have tried to take into consideration learners with diverse abilities and learning styles. Not all activities are meant for all students. A teacher who knows the abilities of the class can select lessons with the learners in mind, choosing activities that will challenge but not overwhelm the kids. The lessons here do not indicate a specific grade level, but rather a range of grades because the abilities of students vary from class to class, school to school, and so forth. A classroom of fifth graders in one school might participate successfully in the mock trial that is described in Chapter 6, but in another school it would be better suited for the seventh grade class.

When selecting a lesson to use, I suggest that attention first be paid to the "Focus," which states the main objective. Second, read through the detailed description of the lesson to determine if your kids are ready for the type of activity that is described. The third consideration is the time element. Some lessons are divided into several sessions and would not be suitable for a fifty-minute time slot.

As a teacher selecting these lessons, please consider the spirit in which they were written. They are suggestions, not written in stone, ideas for lessons that you can adapt to fit your teaching style and change to make your own. Here are my suggestions:

- Choose lessons based on the needs of your students and that you feel are important to their literacy development.
- Choose lessons that attract you and ones that you would feel comfortable teaching.
- Use these lessons as an inspiration to create your own lessons.
- Adapt the lessons as needed to fit the needs of your learners.
- Select your own resources (rather than my suggestions) if they are familiar and readily available.
- Select lessons from Chapter 2 to lay the groundwork for participating in the activities in subsequent chapters.
- Participate in the process and share your enthusiasm and love for language arts.

How This Book Is Organized

The lessons presented here are a result of my own teaching of language arts in elementary and middle school, and as a drama specialist. The first chapter (Setting the Stage for Active Learning) explains the rationale behind this approach, gives detailed descriptions of the strategies that are used throughout the book, and suggests management tips for using them as a venue for learning.

Chapter 2 (Warm-ups for Active Learning) contains lessons that will help prepare the kids for learning through participation. They are recommended to build cooperation, confidence, and concentration, and foster mutual respect at the start of the school year. These lessons, some of which have a game format, are the building blocks for skills that are needed in the chapters that follow.

The subsequent chapters can be used in any order. Chapter 3 (Games and Activities to Enhance Language Learning) contains lessons that are designed to teach writing and enrich vocabulary. They can be accomplished in one teaching session. Chapter 4 (Activities to Promote an Understanding of Story Elements) focuses on using a variety of strategies that promote an understanding of story elements such as plot structure, character conventions, setting, mood, theme, dialogue, and narration. These lessons connect reading with writing.

Many of the lessons in Chapters 5 and 6 take more than one teaching session to accomplish. Chapter 5 (Activities to Develop Oral Language and Reading Fluency) uses literature as an inspiration for a variety of performance readings that develop oral language skills, reading fluency, comprehension of the plot, and an understanding of character. Chapter 6 (Language Arts Performance Projects) contains projects that require an extended period of time to prepare, rehearse, and perform. Literature is the springboard for these performance pieces that involve research, reading, writing, and speaking skills. A focus is cited for each lesson but in these performance projects, all the language arts components of reading, writing, speaking, and listening are synthesized.

A Balanced Approach

By sharing these lessons with fellow teachers, it is my hope that you will try some of them with your class. These strategies have worked for me, and certainly the kids love the time they spend actively participating in this kind of learning. As teachers we need to continue to experiment for effective ways to develop language arts literacy. There needs to be a balance between pencil and paper tasks and participatory learning. This is especially true at this time with the increased focus on testing and retesting our students. As teachers, it is more important than ever to find the time to let our children's voices be heard and valued for their self-expression.

1 Setting the Stage for Active Learning

If you step into my classroom, you will likely see students working in small groups. They are talking, moving, making decisions, and generally cooperating with each other. They appear relaxed as they participate in their learning. It was not always this way. As a first-year teacher, I worried that I wouldn't have enough prepared material to fill the day in a series of directed lessons. In the years that followed, I gradually stepped back and let my students become more involved and take responsibility for their learning. My classroom became a workshop where students participated in authentic acts of reading, writing, speaking, and listening.

In this atmosphere, the students might play the "Mystery Words" game (Chapter 3) as a way to increase their vocabulary. They might create and perform poetry in "Fractured Nursery Rhymes" (Chapter 3) as a means to gain an understanding of rhyme and meter. They might participate in a Readers Theatre (Chapter 5) to improve their reading fluency or role-play a character from literature to improve their literary analysis skills (Chapter 4). All these activities and many more that are described in these lessons are ways to engage students, teach language arts skills, and enrich learning.

Why Active Learning Is an Effective Strategy in Language Arts Teaching

My kids love the time they spend involved in hands-on learning. They are active participants and find it stimulating as well as motivating. But these lessons are more than just appealing. They teach many of the language arts skills that meet the standards, and they provide a way of learning that accommodates a variety of learner styles and intelligences. These lessons reinforce concepts as students put them into action in authentic acts of speaking, writing, reading, and listening.

By using a wide range of activities in language arts learning, it is possible to meet the needs of varied learning styles and abilities. Not all learners are confident or motivated to write and read, but when the goal of writing and reading is to prepare an interview with a character or organize a talk show, a Readers Theatre, or a courtroom trial, then the writing and reading become real and the kids are excited about it.

Lessons That Support the Language Arts Curriculum

The lessons in this book are not add-ons to the language arts curriculum. For me, they have always been an integral part of my teaching of language arts. I have used them in my class to introduce a variety of concepts (for example, a writer's mini-lesson on the topic of character development). At times they are used to provide a lead-in or follow-up to a reading mini-lesson. They can be a culminating activity for literature study or a writing experience (poetry, for example). In essence, all the lessons in this book integrate an essential skill in reading, writing, speaking, or listening.

Many of the lessons, especially those that involve dramatic readings, *improve reading fluency, expression, and comprehension of the text*. The repetitive reading has a purpose—to rehearse for a performance. During the rehearsal process, the actors practice reading with expression. They give attention to punctuation. They learn to articulate and pronounce each word correctly. A script for a Readers Theatre, a TV news program, a radio show, a choral poetry reading, and a play are examples of activities that provide repetitive reading practice.

The games and drama activities also provide an opportunity for *spontaneous oral composition*. Whether it's one line or an entire scene, the kids make it up as they go along. The improvised oral composition helps students with written composition by giving them practice creating a storyline and dialogue. Dramatic play can provide the oral rehearsal for writing a fictional story or a play script.

Speaking skills are improved when children have regular experiences in activities that involve the use of oral language in a structured experience (choral reading, Readers Theatre, enactments, improvised scenes, etc.). The kids develop an awareness of vocal qualities such as articulation, inflection, projection, variety in volume, rate, tone, pitch, and the use of stress and emphasis. As they experience using their voices, they also learn to *communicate through body language and movement*. Children need practice coordinating words with gestures and facial expression. They practice this coordination when they become a character from a book or an invented character. Playing these characters allows the learners to move and gesture unconsciously because they are portraying someone other than themselves.

Many of the lessons in this book are designed to *strengthen listening skills*. Through the varied activities, the children regularly experience listening to respond to cues, to react to another player, to solve problems, to formulate questions, to imagine, and to understand a story (read-aloud books) or a play script. Repeated experiences in oral language work in tandem with the listening experiences. To participate in these hands-on activities, kids quickly learn that it's critical to be an active listener.

These lessons also *promote an understanding of the structural elements of literature* (plot, setting, character, theme, mood, or atmosphere, for example). By teaching literary elements, we teach kids how literature works, and we better enable them to utilize this knowledge in their own writing. In some of the lessons included here, the learners recreate scenes from literature. This is a powerful way to learn about the form and structure of a story. In the planning for the re-creation, I ask questions related to the setting, the mood, theme, and the characters. By becoming characters from a story, experiencing the plot, and creating a setting and mood through dramatic interpretation, the students move toward an understanding of the basic elements of literature. The drama experience takes them from the abstract idea of plot, character, setting, mood, and theme to a concrete experience with these elements, and a better understanding of these concepts.

Finding the Time for Games, Activities, and Performance Projects

The use of games, drama, Readers Theatre, improvisation, and so forth in the language arts classroom is not new. Many teachers utilize one or more of these strategies to teach language skills, and other teachers that I have encountered express reluctance as to how they can fit activities and projects such as the ones in this book into the daily language arts lessons. I understand their skepticism. The daily schedule is tight. These lessons, however, integrate easily into any strand of the language arts curriculum. They are another way for children to learn the subject matter through actively participating in their learning. When I teach the idea of sequencing, for example, I use the lesson "Simple Action Pantomime" (Chapter 3). To help students develop their ability to predict, I use the lesson "You End It" (Chapter 4). To enhance students' ability to use inferencing skills, the lesson from Chapter 4 entitled "Exploring Characterization" works well.

Creating a Classroom Environment for Active Learning

When a new class of students arrives in September, I focus on assessing their social skills. I observe them in the classroom, at recess, in the cafeteria, and in the halls, making mental notes of their behavior. As I watch them, I'm thinking of how to prepare the group to function as a productive class. Experienced teachers know that unless social skills are in place, the chance of a classroom functioning as a successful environment for learning is minimal. This is especially true in the intermediate and middle grades where students spend a lot of time and energy trying to look "cool" in front of their peers. In a classroom where students are participating in games, drama, theatre, and many other hands-on activities, a positive social atmosphere is essential. A good part of language arts learning in my class is done in collaborative groups, so developing a sense of community, trust, respect, and shared responsibility is a primary goal as we begin the school year.

Establishing a Sense of Mutual Respect

Every student needs to know that he or she has respect from his or her peers and from the teacher. If the atmosphere in a classroom is one of mutual respect, then the kids will participate willingly and share their ideas knowing that their peers will not laugh. The expectation is that all students will respect the effort that each student makes to arrive at a solution to a problem.

A respectful classroom atmosphere does not come easily. It needs constant work to establish and then to maintain it throughout the year. Giving time and attention to social skills will set the stage for productive learning. Persistence is important. It takes time out of a lesson to stop and deal with misbehaviors. If inappropriate behavior is not addressed in a positive manner, it will continue. The success of the activities described in these lessons is dependent upon learners who can work as an ensemble or in cooperative groups. Chapter 2 includes many lessons that encourage student cooperation and respect.

Arranging the Physical Space

Each year it seems to me that my classroom is shrinking even though the dimensions remain the same. Computers take a lot of space, as do work stations and a library area. I've had to fight to maintain an open area where my students can all meet for discussions, read-aloud books, story-telling, and numerous games, activities, and project presentations. The space is important. In this area we sit close together. We have a sense of community. There are no desks to separate us. We are close enough to make eye contact and to experience the warmth of smiles and laughter. This intimacy is essential in any group collaboration. My students know that when they sit in our open space they need to be ready to listen. They anticipate that exciting things will happen there.

Our open area has a prop shelf at one end. On this shelf are some simple props (cups, dishes, magazines, newspapers, purses, briefcase, jewelry box, an assortment of fake food, etc.) and a few costume pieces (aprons, shawls, capes, hats, jackets, tunics, etc.). The use of props and costumes is introduced gradually as students become comfortable working in this space.

Promoting a Comfortable and Productive Climate for Learning

Experienced teachers know that the teacher's attitude can influence the learning atmosphere. If I want my kids to be respectful, for example, then I need to model it. A few strategies for creating a positive classroom atmosphere conducive to hands-on learning that have worked for me are the following:

- I try to be supportive and handle negative behavior in a positive manner.

- I show my enthusiasm for the lesson. Enthusiasm is contagious. The kids know when you really love what you are doing and they want to be a part of it.

- I am a careful listener. I focus on possibilities for helping students by asking skilled questions. Thought-provoking questions help students discover approaches or solutions to the problems presented.

- I work to find the strong points in each of my students and I capitalize on those.

Management Strategies for an Active Classroom

If you have ever watched kids pass through the door on the way to a recess, then you have witnessed an electrifying burst of energy as they bolt onto the playground, smiling and yelling to each other. Kids love being active. So the question arises, "While my students are involved in active learning in the classroom, how can I avoid having the classroom sound like the recess yard?" I think that most teachers work on this on a regular basis while teaching daily lessons. The same cues and ground rules that we use when children work at their desks or tables also work in the open learning area.

Nevertheless groups need to be organized, expectations need to be clear, and a structure needs to be in place for each activity. Following are a few management tips that have worked in my classroom during active sessions.

Taking a Serious Approach

I keep my attitude businesslike as I introduce and facilitate the activities. I want to convey to my kids that their participation in the games and so forth is another way to learn a subject, not a time for a recess. By handling the time spent participating in these active lessons as seriously as I would handle a math or science lesson, the idea of a "drama recess" slowly fades and in its place is the idea of a work space that is an alternative area to their desks and pencil and paper tasks.

Making Expectations Clear

I make my expectations clear for social behavior. A quick reminder before we start a session usually keeps behavior on track. I expect good listeners. I expect that they will show respect to their peers and me (students know what this heavily packed word called *respect* means in real examples because we have invested a lot of time understanding the impact of the word). I expect cooperation while working in groups, and that each student will make the best possible effort to find appropriate solutions to the problems presented.

Participating in the Activities

I participate in many of the lessons for several reasons. At the start of the year I lead many of the games to model how they are played. When the kids feel comfortable with them and know the rules, then I choose a student to lead. Also, I feel that if I ask my kids to perform, then I should be willing to do it myself. The same attitude prevails when I teach writing. If I expect my kids to participate in the arduous process of writing, then I should be willing to work on my own writing and share my difficulties and successes.

Giving Clear Directions and Establishing Cues

My oral directions are clear and to the point (Typical examples: Sit cross-legged on the drama circle. Find your own space. Eyes on me. Listen for my stop signal). If the activity is complicated and involves groups that are preparing a presentation, then a "What You Need to Do" list is posted and a deadline is suggested. Knowing the deadline keeps the groups working productively during the planning session.

I teach students the cues that I plan to use as signals to start or stop. I use the same cues in every session. Perhaps the most important cue word is the one that signals them to stop. I use the word *freeze.* Any word or sound effect can be used as long as all the kids know that when they hear it, it means all action stops and there is immediate silence. At the start of the year, we practice responding to the cue by walking around the class, then freezing when I give the cue. I use other signals to start and stop the action in any performance piece. The word *curtain* is used to signal that the action should begin, and again the word *curtain* signals that the scene should end. It really doesn't matter what cue is used. What matters is the response to the cue.

Focusing on Success

I emphasize what my kids are doing right rather than focus on what they're doing wrong. For example, if a group is performing a tableau (a living picture) and one student is unfocused, then I look for those students who are focused and compliment them (for example: "I like the way Mary and Billy are concentrating. I'm getting a clear picture of the action.").

While performing, if a student engages in "horseplay" to get attention, my response to the silly behavior might be something like this: I ask the student to recall the problem or task that was given at the outset of the activity to be sure that the assignment was understood. As I ask a series of questions designed to help the student self-evaluate, it becomes evident to the student that the horseplay was not a valid response to the problem presented. By handling negative behavior in this way, the *focus is put on the activity rather than on the child's behavior*. I give the student a chance to rethink the response and come up with an alternative solution. Usually success is achieved the second time around.

Planning Each Session Carefully

A productive session that involves active learning is one that is carefully planned. I schedule the block of time needed for the activity and prepare any materials needed for the lesson. I have a clear objective in mind and share this purpose with the students at the start of the lesson.

Involving All the Students

At the start of the school year, I schedule lessons in my open space involving all the students in large group work. Everyone is working in unison and no one is waiting for a turn. It is during the "downtime" that students get off task. Also, when everyone is working together, students feel more confident. The spotlight is not on one person, but on everyone.

When I begin small group and partnered activities, then it's time to have a discussion about the *role of the audience*. I explain that even though the audience is sitting and watching, it has an active role. While a group is presenting, the audience's involvement centers on being *polite listeners* and *evaluative listeners*. Often I give a viewing purpose by posting a few questions for discussion after each performance. (Example: Did the group solve the problem presented? Was the setting revealed? How did the actors reveal the setting to the audience?) By using this approach, the *discussion focuses on the solution to the problem* that the kids were solving rather than on the actors who performed in the presentation.

Types of Activities Used in the Lessons

The lessons in this book incorporate a variety of hands-on activities to teach language arts. I know that teachers will recognize some of them. Games, read-aloud books, Readers Theatre, debating, and public speaking are often used in the classroom. Teachers have less familiarity with activities such as pantomime, improvisation, tableaux, and enactment. Terminology that might need some clarification is defined here.

Read-Aloud Books

Although many teachers use read-aloud books regularly, the use becomes less frequent as students move into the higher grades, and yet it can be a very helpful strategy. In fifth grade I regularly use picture books to teach lessons; I have even used them with my college students. Before I begin a lesson, I show the students the picture book (some might be familiar with the title) and I explain to the kids why I am using it for the lesson. Once they understand the rationale, they sit back, relax, and enjoy the experience of hearing a story that reminds them of their happy days in the primary grades.

Games

As teachers we are familiar with games as a learning tool and a means of recreation. Games present an opportunity for emotional and social growth. Through games children develop confidence, concentration, and group awareness. Games strengthen communication skills when students observe, experience, and react to others and to situations. Through participation in games, the learners practice cooperation and discipline. Games are used frequently in Chapters 2 and 3 to provide an opportunity for social growth. The effectiveness of the games depends on the leader (the teacher) who explains and directs the game. The leader makes sure that the players respect the rules and each other.

Pantomime

Pantomime is a means of conveying ideas through movement, gesture, and expression rather than in words. Pantomime can be as simple as a single gesture (wrinkling the nose in reaction to a bad smell), or complex with a series of detailed movements (making a bed). Pantomime is the prologue to improvisation. When students are successful expressing meaning with their bodies, the natural next step is to add words to the dramatization.

Structuring pantomime in large groups is an ideal strategy for developing confidence in learners. Students are focused on movement and expression without the additional burden of creating dialogue.

In my role as the leader, I incorporate ideas into the lessons that are relevant to my kids' lives. Eating an ice cream cone and doing homework are familiar activities to my learners, but driving a bus or working as a bank teller are out of the realm of their experience.

To assure success in pantomime activities (or any hands-on experience), I act as a coach by talking and asking questions *while* students perform. In theatre terminology, this is called *side-coaching*. It is a useful strategy to stimulate new ideas as players work to solve a problem. Teachers engage in this style of coaching on a daily basis in the form of questions that they ask students during an activity. In science, for example, as a teacher facilitates during an experiment, productive questions are frequently used to generate new ideas. Although the term *side-coaching* might be new, the process is not new to teachers. In the pantomime example of eating the ice cream cone, my *side-coaching* questions might be the following: Is it a sunny day? Is the cone melting? Do you bite or lick the cone? Do you eat slowly or quickly? How can you show the texture of the cone? Is it one, two, or three scoops? *Side-coaching* encourages students to develop detailed pantomimes because the questioning puts the focus on the *process,* not just the solution.

Tableau

A tableau is a living picture (like people captured in a moment of time in a photo). In the classroom, groups of students create frozen positions to depict a scene from a story. The living pictures are carefully prepared to communicate an idea from the text. Gesture, expression, body position, focus, and energy are all considered during the planning stage. In my experience using this strategy, I have found it to be effective in promoting comprehension of story structure, characterizations, and setting.

Choral Reading

In this activity, students read (or recite from memory) the same text. It is read aloud with variations of speakers and vocal techniques. Choral reading is prevalent in primary grades and used less frequently in the upper grades. This is unfortunate because I've observed older kids involved in the experience and they love it. Due to the communal effort, all the readers (even the struggling ones) are successful. After several practices, the performers are reading the text smoothly. There are solos and duets, pauses and crescendos, and gestures and facial expressions to create interest for the listener during the reading (see Chapter 5 for suggestions on staging a reading). Poetry or any short texts are good choices for a choral reading.

Enactment (Story Dramatization)

In this activity, students act out a story, adhering closely to the author's plot and the dialogue used by the characters in the text. In other words, the actors try to bring to life the words of the author.

Enactments take careful planning. After a decision is made to enact a scene from a book (or the entire book if the text is short), the scene is outlined to determine the major plot actions, the setting, and the characters. Using the outline as a motivation, the actors begin the scene. Scripts are not used and most of the dialogue is *improvised*. Occasionally, the actors use a line directly from the text, especially if it is key to the meaning of the story (for example: "Mirror, mirror on the wall, who's the fairest of them all?"). The dramatization is repeated several times. During each repetition, more details are added, dialogue is refined, and a sense of place (setting) emerges. If time allows, students work on improving their voices. Props and a few simple costume pieces are added to suggest their characters. In Chapter 5, there are several detailed examples of enactments.

Improvisation

In theatre, the term *improvisation* refers to a *spontaneous creation* by the actors. No scripts are involved. Improvisations take many forms. A pantomime could be improvised. A single line ("One-Line Improvisation with a Prop," Chapter 2) or spontaneous movement ("Introductions," Chapter 2) could also be termed improvisation. In Chapter 4, "On-the-Scene Reporter" takes an impromptu interview format.

Even though the term *spontaneous* is used here, it is important to note that many improvisations need careful planning (like a good piece of writing that is the result of a step-by-step process). To create a scene, the actors need a main idea or conflict. Scenes must have a beginning, middle, and an end. Character relationships need to be clear to the audience. Movement around the playing area is blocked out so all the actors are visible. "You End It" (Chapter 4) and "Enacting Scenes from Literature" (Chapter 5) utilize the improvisational process to create scenes.

Readers Theatre

Readers Theatre is now popular as a teaching strategy across the curriculum in many classrooms. Unlike conventional theatre, in Readers Theatre the actors read rather than memorize scripts. They use their voices to interpret and communicate a story or informational content to the audience. The emphasis is on spoken words rather than on movement, scenery, lighting, costumes, and so forth.

In many classrooms, Readers Theatre is an opportunity to read a prepared script from published or Internet resources. By doing so, oral language, fluency, confidence, and motivation are enhanced. However, I believe that Readers Theatre has greater potential as a learning strategy if the participants create their own scripts. By doing so, the learners synthesize reading, writing, speaking, listening, and curriculum content into the performance preparation. Chapter 5 includes details on adapting literature for Readers Theatre and also on writing original scripts for a Readers Theatre.

Scripted Drama

Scripted drama is a performance that follows a written script that is memorized or sometimes read by the actors. Chapter 6 has examples of scripted performances ("TV News Show" and "Writing in Role").

Figure 1–1   Students in colonial costume await the "courtroom trial" of Captain Preston

Debating

In debating, students choose a side *for* or *against* a proposition and prepare arguments to support their side of the issue. Writing, reading, speaking (sometimes extemporaneous), listening, and critical thinking are skills that are combined in debating. If the debate is between literary or historical characters, then role-playing is needed. The debate becomes a dramatic performance. Chapter 6 includes a lesson using this strategy.

Courtroom Trial

Students participate in a mock trial acting as lawyers, witnesses, jurors, judge, and the accused. They use trial procedures in the drama as they prepare statements, arguments, cross-examination questions, and rebuttals. Trials can involve fictional characters from literature (for example, *The Wicked Witch v. Snow White*) or characters from historical trials (example: John Adams' defense of Captain Preston). Chapter 6 includes a lesson using a courtroom trial, as shown in Figure 1–1.

Interview

Students take on the role of reporters by preparing questions to ask in a face-to-face interview. The person being interviewed (real or fictional) is asked to express opinions or share background information. In "On-the-Scene Reporter" (Chapter 4), students interview fairy tale and nursery rhyme characters caught up in a conflict. To prepare for "A Meeting of the Historical Society" (Chapter 6), students interview a family member or relative. In "Talk Show Host" (Chapter 6), characters from a novel appear together on a talk show and are interviewed by the host.

Writing in Role

In this activity, the writers step into the shoes of another and share the feelings and ideas of a character from a book. The first-person narrative takes the form of a monologue, diary entries, or a letter. In Chapter 6, there is a lesson that uses this strategy.

Using the Lessons in This Book

I suggest in the introduction that teachers choose lessons from this book that they feel comfortable teaching. If your background is limited in drama, then you might want to choose some of the traditional games or activities such as debating, interviewing, choral reading, and storytelling. However, each lesson in the book describes the activity in great detail, making it possible for a teacher who enjoys using a hands-on approach to successfully implement any of the lessons.

For teachers who are interested in widening their knowledge base in drama as a teaching strategy, or learning more about performance projects such as Readers Theatre, storytelling, and story dramatization, the "Recommended Professional Reading" at the end of this book might be helpful.

2 Warm-ups for Active Learning

During the first few months of the school year, I strive to have my kids feel relaxed and confident while participating in active learning. I want them to feel the same comfort level that they experience playing a game during physical education, singing in a music class, or sharing their work in the art room. It's important that the kids feel safe as they perform with or for the group. To develop the social skills that are needed to participate successfully, I suggest that the activities in this chapter be used to lay the groundwork for lessons in other chapters.

The chapter begins with an ice-breaker activity called "Introductions." This is a circle game played with the entire class that focuses on group awareness and building confidence. Some lessons are based on *traditional games* ("Who Started the Motion?" "Get in Line," "Who Am I?"), and they have a goal of developing what I call the "3 C's": *confidence, cooperation,* and *concentration*. By playing these games, the kids learn that game playing is an authentic way to learn in the classroom. The games build group awareness and cooperative work skills. The learners are moving unconsciously with their bodies and developing confidence with their physical presence. These games are the building blocks to develop the skills that are necessary in the lessons that follow.

Another way to strengthen the students' confidence, cooperation, and concentration is through *pantomime* activities. Pantomime allows the participants to express themselves through body movement, facial expression, and gesture without having the additional burden of speaking. A group pantomime activity such as "Safety in Numbers" establishes the confidence that is needed for more challenging activities that require the use of improvised dialogue and scripts. Other lessons in the chapter combine oral and written language ("Mystery Object" and "Marooned") to practice speaking and descriptive writing skills.

These introductory lessons establish a positive social atmosphere, one that is marked by discipline and seriousness in approach. I recommend that time be taken to teach many of the lessons in this chapter, choosing them with the needs of your group in mind. Once routines and expectations are established, students feel comfortable and are ready to participate in the lessons of the following chapters.

··

INTRODUCTIONS

Focus

Played with the entire class, this activity develops confidence and group awareness.

Grade Levels: 3–8

Purpose

This is an excellent get-acquainted game that I usually introduce on the first day of school. Players learn the names of their classmates and I learn the names of my students. It eases nervousness that kids feel in a new situation.

Benefits
- develops confidence
- encourages spontaneity
- builds group awareness

Materials Needed: None

Description of the Activity

After I organize the students in a large circle, we discuss their favorite pastimes (sports, hobbies, lessons, etc.). Then I ask each player to decide on one pastime to have in mind when we play the game.

I direct all the players to stand and I explain how the game is played, "When it is your turn, say your name, then say and pantomime your favorite pastime. Everyone will then repeat your words and actions." I go on to demonstrate what I mean to reinforce my directions, "My name is Ms. Fennessey, and I love to swim" (pantomime the action of swimming). I then direct the group to mimic me by saying, "Her name is Ms. Fennessey and she loves to swim" (the entire group pantomimes swimming). Following the directions and the practice, I ask for a volunteer to start the game. The first player starts (for example, "My name is Tyler and I play baseball"), then the group repeats his name and imitates Tyler's action. The player to Tyler's right continues by stating her name and an action (for example, "My name is

Priscilla and I like soccer"), and the group mimics her action. The game continues until everyone in the circle has had a turn. It is possible to go around several times. I suggest that the players pick a new action for their pantomime or change to another pastime for the new round.

In an advanced version of this game, one player starts by saying a name and pantomiming an action, then the player to the right repeats what the first player said and did, then adds a new name and action. The third player then repeats the words and actions of player one, player two, and then adds a name and action. The game continues until it reaches the last player who must repeat the name and action of everyone in the group, then add a name and action. If you have a large group, it is possible to modify the game by having the players repeat only the last four players' names and actions.

Teacher-to-Teacher

Students have no difficulty thinking of something that they love to do when they are not in school. By having the group imitate each player's words and actions, all the players must listen carefully and focus on each player as the game moves around the circle.

....

WHO STARTED THE MOTION?

Focus

This lesson focuses on developing group cooperation, confidence, and observational skills.

Grade Levels: 3–8

Purpose

This traditional children's game has been played for many years. It's a simple yet very effective way to build group awareness and interaction among students. As the kids participate in the fun of playing this observational game, they are unconsciously moving with their bodies and developing confidence with their physical presence.

Benefits
- develops confidence and cooperation
- builds group awareness
- improves observational skills

Materials Needed: None

Description of the Activity

The students stand in a circle in an open space in the classroom. I ask for a volunteer to be "it." The student who is "it" leaves the room. Another player is chosen to be the leader who makes the motions. The leader begins an action that all the other players imitate. Then "it" is asked to return to the room and stand in the center of the circle to determine who is leading the group. "It" observes the group carefully trying to catch the leader initiating a motion. "It" has three guesses. When "it" guesses correctly, the game begins again with a new student who is "it." If the player does not guess correctly, the leader is revealed and a new "it" is chosen to go out of the room to restart the game.

Teacher-to-Teacher

I use games consistently as a teaching strategy with both my fifth graders and my college students. By watching the participants, I learn a great deal about them. Any age group can play this game. Older students are adept in using strategies to conceal the leader. With younger students, I lead a discussion on how to watch and imitate the motions of the leader without making it obvious. We also discuss strategies that will help the student who is "it" make a correct guess.

It's important for the teacher to model the role of the leader in this game. When I lead, I try to use my body in a variety of motions that incorporate the head, shoulders, arms, hands, hips, legs, and feet. The child who lacks the confidence to lead the group through the motions will get ideas by watching other students and me as we lead the group.

....

GET IN LINE

Focus

This lesson develops cooperation, concentration, and observational skills.

Grade Levels: 3–8

Purpose

Being a keen observer is an important trait to promote in a developing writer. Observing the way people walk, talk, and make gestures provides descriptive detail for the writer to create believable characters. Observing surroundings accurately helps the writer to describe a setting. This game sharpens the learner's accuracy when observing.

Benefits
- improves observational skills
- develops group cooperation

Materials Needed: None

Description of the Activity

We sit in a circle in our open space in the classroom. I pick five or six students at random. These students are instructed to leave the classroom and quickly organize themselves in a single file, then return in that formation to the center of the circle. The students in the circle are instructed to observe their formation carefully and remember it. After a few seconds, those in the line quickly leave the room, change their formation in the line, and then come back into the room in a single file to the center of the circle. The observers, taking turns, try to rearrange the line back to its original formation. (*Note:* There are two ways to do this. The observers can orally instruct the players to move to a position in the line; or two or three students could be appointed to come to the center and move the students in the line back to their original position.) When the observers think that they have put the line back to its original order, the players respond by confirming that the order is correct, or by making the needed adjustments to the line.

Teacher-to-Teacher

I play observational games with the students throughout the entire year. I make sure that young writers understand the connection between being a keen observer and being a skilled writer. I give homework assignments that focus on observation. For example, I might ask the kids to write a detailed description of a portion of their bedroom or observe the way family members walk and try to describe their various gaits.

....

WHO AM I?

Focus

This game develops questioning skills and self-confidence. It is loosely based on the parlor game "Twenty Questions."

Grade Levels: 3–8

Purpose

When students are new to each other at the start of the school year, it's important for them to participate in ice-breaker activities that involve the entire class. These activities allow the students to develop confidence in front of their peers in a nonthreatening way and prepare them for language arts performance projects.

Benefits

- builds group cooperation and group awareness
- gives practice formulating questions
- strengthens concentration

Materials Needed

- name tags, each printed with a different name of a well-known literary character selected with the students' knowledge-base in mind (for example: Cinderella, Snow White, Peter Pan, Little Red Riding Hood, Harry Potter, Stuart Little, Wilbur [*Charlotte's Web*], Alice in Wonderland, Big Bad Wolf, Cat in the Hat, Dorothy [*The Wizard of Oz*], Goldilocks, Sleeping Beauty, Pinocchio, Captain Hook, Rapunzel, Rumpelstiltskin, Winnie-the-Pooh, a main character from *Chronicles of Narnia*, Little Miss Muffet, Little Bo Peep)

Description of the Activity

At the start of the session, I explain the purpose of the game: students need to guess their identity by asking questions. Players are allowed to ask only questions that can be answered with a "yes" or a "no." I attach a name tag (self-sticking type) on the back of each student, being careful not to let the student see the name. It will be visible to others, but not to the student who is wearing the name tag. The tag has the name of a famous person from literature, a fairy tale, a folk tale, a classic, and so on.

Next, I ask each student to find an individual space somewhere in the room. When I say, "Go!" the students walk randomly around the room and stop to ask a question of another student (example: Am I a woman?). After students have each asked one question, they move on to another student to ask another question. They continue on until they have questioned every student in the group and then start over if needed. If a student, however, wants to make a guess at the identity of the character, he or she says, "I think I am (name of the character)." If the student is correct, that student sits down to become an observer until all players know their identity. If the student is incorrect, then the questioning continues.

Teacher-to-Teacher

This game can be lively and fun, but it is much more than that. It involves the use of critical thinking skills as students formulate questions to discover their identity. This type of activity sets the stage for more advanced whole group activities such as "The Talk Show" or "On-the-Scene Reporter."

During the random walk, I suggest that students use "whispers only" as the means of communication. As the facilitator, I watch carefully to make sure that they don't give hints to each other. Also, if there are students who experience difficulty making an identification, I help them generate questions that narrow down the possibilities, or pick character identities for those students that can be more easily identified.

SAFETY IN NUMBERS

Focus

This all-class pantomime activity develops confidence and awareness of setting.

Grade Levels: 3–8

Purpose

Pantomime is an excellent way to ease kids into drama activities. They express themselves through body movement, facial expression, and gesture without having the additional burden of creating dialogue. Making a situation believable requires concentration as the players try to make a place or character real to the audience. Group pantomime provides safety for students who lack confidence. It is also a natural lead-in to individual work and scenes with dialogue.

Benefits
- develops an awareness of setting
- builds confidence, cooperation, and concentration
- prepares students for speech-related activities

Figure 2–1   Students participate in the pantomime game, "Safety in Numbers."

Materials Needed
- index cards with familiar places and situations printed on them (see the list of suggested settings at the end of this lesson)

Description of the Activity

I divide students into workable groups of four to six students. (See Figure 2–1.) I explain to all the students that the focus of the pantomime is to make the setting believable to the audience. Their movement, posture, gestures, facial expression, and interaction with the other players should convey the setting and the situation.

I give an index card to each group and suggest that they find a space to plan their pantomime. After five minutes we are ready to begin. One group sets up the playing area with the needed furniture (for example, several chairs, a table, or a bench). The remaining groups take their place in the audience. At this point, I give the audience a *viewing purpose*. I might say, "Watch the scene to determine the setting. Ask yourself, what actions or gestures of the actors helped reveal the setting? If you know the setting, please do not call it out. Wait until the actors have finished the scene, then raise your hand." Each group takes a turn performing. After each pantomime, I restate the viewing purpose and the students share their thoughts. If there is time, a new round of cards is distributed and the players once again take turns performing. At any time during a performance, I might interject a question to suggest additional solutions for the scene. For example, if the students were depicting the scene at the school bus stop, I might say, "How can you reveal to the audience that it is early morning?"

Teacher-to-Teacher

I use this activity every year as a confidence booster, especially for my ESL students. Through pantomime they experiment unself-consciously, and it motivates them to participate in other activities that require speech later in the year.

Choosing settings that are familiar to your students is an important factor that determines the success of this activity. City kids have experiences with settings that are different from children who live in the suburbs or rural areas. I suggest that settings be chosen with that in mind. Here are some settings that have worked for me:

- waiting at the school bus stop in the morning
- watching a scary movie in the theatre
- eating pizza in a pizza place with teammates after a game
- waiting in the dentist's office
- watching a school soccer game in the bleachers
- researching in the library
- girls (boys) in the bedroom at a sleepover party
- snacking while watching television in the living room
- moving through the cafeteria counter line at school
- eating ice cream in the park
- waiting to cross a busy street
- raking leaves in the yard
- walking around in a museum
- riding on a bus during a field trip
- making a sandcastle on the beach
- eating hamburgers in a fast food restaurant
- hiking in the woods
- window shopping in a mall or on a street

SENSORY GAMES

Focus

The three games presented here focus on using sensory detail in writing.

Grade Levels: 3–5

Purpose

Professional writers use sensory detail to create a picture in the reader's mind, but young writers often lack the skills needed to use this strategy. They first need to develop an *awareness of the meaning of sensory detail*. Secondly, they need to build a collection of *vocabulary words* that are specific to the senses. These games on touching, hearing, and tasting heighten their awareness of how writers use sensory detail and they expand the use of specific sensory vocabulary.

Benefits

- develops an awareness of how sensory detail is used in writing
- increases the use of sensory vocabulary in writing
- provides an oral rehearsal for the learner who is describing objects that are touched, sounds that are heard, and food that is tasted

Materials Needed

- touch game: a variety of objects (a different one for each student) with varying shapes, textures, and sizes
- hearing game: a variety of objects that can be used to make sounds (scratching on a chalkboard, cutting paper, opening a drawer, turning a pencil sharpener, etc.); blindfolds for each student
- tasting game: trays with bite-size pieces of food in that have a variety of tastes and textures (for example: potato chip, pretzel, cracker, green apple, pickle, lemon, sour ball, chocolate chip, miniature marshmallow, cookie, carrot stick, watermelon, banana, Fruit Loop™); blindfolds for each student

Description of Sensory Game 1: Identify the Object Through Touch

Ahead of time, I gather a variety of objects with varying shapes, textures, and sizes (small enough to fit in cupped hands). There should be a different one for each student. The students sit cross-legged in a circle. I explain that they will need to identify an object using only their sense of touch. My instructions might be as follows: "When I give the signal, you need to look straight ahead and cup your hands behind your back. I will place an object in everyone's hands. Through your sense of touch, you will need to describe the size, shape, texture, weight, the type of material of the object, and if there are any moving parts. You will be disqualified from the game if you look at your object or at your neighbor's object."

To start, I walk around the outside of the circle and place an object in each of the students' hands. I call on each player first to describe the shape, size, weight, texture, and so forth of the object and finally to guess what the object might be. A player might say the following: "Its shape is round on one end and thin on the other end, like a handle. The handle part and the outside rim feel like plastic. The round part feels smooth, like glass or maybe a mirror. The glass part is curved, like a dome shape with a rim around it. It's not very heavy, maybe four or five ounces and about five inches long." At this point, I ask the player, "Can you name your object?" The player might correctly guess that it is a magnifying glass. If the player makes a wrong guess, then I ask questions to help the player: "What is the shape? What is the texture? Does it have any moving parts? What material is it made of?" If the student is still puzzled, then I ask the player to reveal the object to the group because the focus of the game is on using descriptive detail to describe what is being touched rather than solely guessing the name of the object. After each player has had a turn, I ask that the object be placed in the center of the circle and we move on to the next player until all students have had a turn.

Description of Sensory Game 2: What Am I Hearing?

This game works well if it is played in a classroom with its variety of objects such as a chalkboard, pencil sharpener, file cabinets, and so forth. I also place additional objects not normally found about the room (for example, tin cans, aluminum foil, plastic packing paper, tambourine, bag of marbles). The students sit cross-legged in a circle. I explain that in this listening game, they need to focus all their energy *hearing* the sound being made, and *thinking of words* to describe the sound, and finally *identifying how the sound is made*. The first time we play this game, I act as the leader with one or two student assistants. When students are more accomplished playing the game, they lead the game themselves.

After giving the instructions, I pass out pieces of cloth to use as blindfolds and tell the students to tie them on. I then ask that there not be any sound or motion in the room so they can concentrate on listening. I move to a place in the classroom (for example, the chalkboard) and make a sound by writing on the board with the chalk. I repeat the sound several times to make sure that everyone has heard the sound clearly. Then I ask, "What are you hearing?" I encourage students to respond in complete sentences, such as: "I heard a scraping sound. I think that it was the sound of chalk on the blackboard"; or "I heard a grinding sound. I think that you were turning the pencil sharpener." I move the game along quickly to give most students a turn guessing or creating sounds for others to guess. At the end, the students remove their blindfolds. At this point, I ask them to recall some of the sounds. I record their responses, making a list to be posted under the title of *Sound Words* (for example: grinding, scratching, crunching, thumping, banging, crackling, grating, clanging, scraping, rolling, tapping, etc.). The more the students play this game, the more acute their listening becomes, and their sensory vocabulary increases.

Description of Sensory Game 3: What Am I Tasting?

Ahead of time I prepare trays with food cut into bite-size pieces for tasting. I think about having a variety of tastes and textures. Examples include the following: salty (potato chip, pretzel, cracker), sour (green apple, pickle, lemon, or a sour ball), sweet (a chocolate chip, miniature marshmallow, cookie, carrot stick, watermelon, banana, a Fruit Loop). As a precaution I make sure that I'm aware of any allergies in my class, and also use a plastic glove to prevent spreading germs.

To start, the players are blindfolded sitting in a circle or at their desks. I ask them to cup one hand in front of their waists. I distribute the various pieces of food and give instructions: "When I tell you to start, carefully place the piece of food in your mouth. Chew slowly and concentrate on its taste and texture. Try to think of words that describe the taste and texture. When I call on you, use a sentence to describe the food you tasted." I continue to encourage the use of complete sentences. A player might say the following: "It has a sour taste with a crunchy texture. It made juice in my mouth. I think that it was a piece of apple." I frequently remind the kids that the focus of this game is to describe the taste rather than guess the name of the food.

Teacher-to-Teacher

Getting the kids to craft sentences using sensory detail is not an easy task. I return to this topic many times during the year in my mini-lessons. We look at excerpts from books by professional authors and students identify the sensory detail. In a read-aloud, I ask students to listen for sensory words and jot down a few examples to share. We create lists to be posted for use during writing sessions. We practice transforming bland sentences into savory ones.

••

ONE-LINE IMPROVISATION WITH A PROP

Focus

This large group improvisational game builds confidence while practicing the coordination of body and voice.

Grade Levels: 3–8

Purpose

At the outset of the year, I use many pantomime activities during drama sessions as a way of developing confidence in the learners. Once they feel safe in the drama circle, we begin to use the body and voice together in short one-line improvisations. A single prop helps to support the child's confidence by focusing the attention *on the prop* and *not on the child*.

Benefits

- coordinates body and voice in self-expression

- enhances listening skills

- promotes creativity in problem-solving activities

- develops confidence when speaking in front of a group

Materials Needed

- a simple prop that is not too specific (a *pole*, for example, about the length of a yardstick can become many things: fishing pole, paddle, baseball bat, handle on a vacuum, magic wand, and so forth; other objects that I've successfully used are a long piece of cloth and an object about the size of a Frisbee™)

Description of the Activity

All the players gather in the drama circle either standing or sitting. I show one object—for example, the pole. I explain to the group, "This object can be anything you want it to be. You are the magician and you can change it into something new as it goes from player to player around the circle. When you get the object, you need to use the object that you have created and say a line that will help the other players identify your object." I then demonstrate. If the object is a pole, I might wave it back and forth across "the ground" as if it were a metal detector, then say, "I know I lost that gold ring here somewhere." Once the players have the idea, the object moves around the circle. Each player transforms it into a new object, improvises a line, and then passes it to the next player. If a player cannot think of an idea, the object passes again. Here are some examples of objects that players have created in the past:

- a magician's wand: "Ladies and gentlemen, watch closely as I wave my magic wand."
- a vacuum: "I'd better clean this up before Mom gets home."
- fishing pole: "I can't even get a bite!"
- toothbrush: "With this toothbrush, I'm guaranteed to have no cavities!"

Teacher-to-Teacher

I emphasize "showing" the object rather than "telling" the viewer what it is. I coach the participants by saying, "Show me how you use it, don't tell me what it is." I also encourage the players to keep the object moving around the circle, not stop while a player thinks of an idea. For those who keep passing the object when it comes to them, I help them by whispering a suggestion for an improvisation. This helps the students work through the initial self-consciousness and usually the next time around, they create their own idea.

TONGUE TWISTERS

Focus

The focus of this lesson is on fluency and articulation in speech.

Grade Levels: 3–5

Purpose

Kids love saying tongue twisters especially when their tongues get twisted and we all have a good laugh. For this reason, tongue twisters are an excellent warm-up or icebreaker activity. Saying them quickly and accurately requires clear and agile movements of the lips, tongue, teeth, and soft palate. Concentration is needed because the reader sees and says the words simultaneously in an oral reading activity. It combines visual, kinesthetic, and auditory modes.

Benefits

- improves articulation and fluency in oral speech
- develops an awareness of the effort needed in the facial muscles to produce clear speech
- increases accuracy in oral reading

Materials Needed

- tongue twisters (see examples in the Teacher-to-Teacher section)
- additional resource: *A Twister of Twists, a Tangler of Tongues* by Alvin Schwartz

Description of the Activity

At the start of the session, I post several tongue twisters on chart paper. We practice in unison saying each five or six times in succession. I start slowly, emphasizing articulation and correct pronunciation. Once students are reading accurately and clearly, I pick up speed, going the fastest on the final repetitions. If students are stumbling when they pick up speed, I make suggestions. If the tongue twister uses the "th" sound (for example: The path threads through the thicket), I show the kids how to hold the tip of their tongue lightly against the inside of the upper front teeth to produce the sound. We advance from short tongue twisters to longer ones. After practicing in unison, students work on a solo presentation or with a partner (some kids might need the support).

Teacher-to-Teacher

After the activity, I lead a discussion with the kids on the usefulness of tongue twisters for warming up the voice and improving the flexibility of the lips, tongue, and soft palate. It's an excellent preparation for a Readers Theatre in which students need to speak fluently, clearly, and accurately to be understood by the audience. Ultimately, I hope that my students begin to recognize the importance of clear speech to communicate an idea to the listener.

The following is a list of *short tongue twisters* that I've used in my lessons.

- toy boat
- rubber baby buggy bumpers

- red leather, yellow leather
- unique New York
- Peggy Babcock
- thirty-three thieves in the thicket
- black bug's blood
- Greek grapes
- a box of mixed biscuits
- red blood, blue blood
- six slippery snails slid slowly seaward
- crisp crusts crackle and crunch
- upper roller, lower roller
- freshly fried flat flying fish
- purple paper people
- shy Shelly says she shall sew sheets shortly
- A big black bug bit a big black bear, made the big black bear bleed blood.
- Betty and Bobby blew big blue bubbles.
- Which wristwatches are Swiss wristwatches?
- Round and round the rugged rock the ragged rascal ran.

MYSTERY OBJECT

Focus

This lesson's goal is to expand descriptive vocabulary.

Grade Levels: 3–8

Purpose

This activity is particularly useful in helping kids expand their descriptive vocabulary. In science, for example, when asked to describe in words what they see under the microscope, children often lack the precise vocabulary needed for a detailed description. Words such as *opaque, coarse, rectangular, spongy,* for example, are unfamiliar to them. This activity promotes the use of a wide variety of descriptive words.

Benefits

- expands the use of specific descriptive vocabulary words that describe shape, texture, size, and density
- develops speaking skills
- increases confidence in front of an audience
- improves dictionary skills

Materials Needed

- a paper bag with an object inside (In my modeling activity, I use a pair of scissors.)
- vocabulary list

Description of the Activity

To facilitate this activity, a day or two before, I pass out a vocabulary list that is organized into categories such as texture words, shape words, and so forth. I ask students to highlight any unfamiliar words. They use dictionaries to find the meanings of those words and record them.

To model the activity, I show the students a brown paper bag and tell them that I have a mystery object inside. I direct them to listen to my description of the object:

> My object is made of shiny silver metal. It's about ten inches long and about an eighth of an inch thick. It has two parts that are held together in the middle by a screw. Each part has an oval shape at one end, and is pointed and sharp at the other end. The tapered metal in between has a sharp blade on one side and is blunt on the other side. It is possible to open and close the two parts. When you do, they scrape together, then make a clicking sound as they close completely.

I end with the closing cue for making guesses: *What is my mystery object?*

For homework, I ask the students to find an object at home that fits into a paper or plastic bag (about lunch size). They write a detailed description of the object using precise words to describe its shape, texture, density, type of material, and so forth. The object is then placed in the bag and taped or stapled to close it.

The next day, we gather in a circle in our open space and all the kids place their bags in front of them. I ask for a volunteer to get the game started. That child either reads or recites from memory the description of the object, then ends with the cue line: "What is my mystery object?" Students make guesses and the one who correctly identifies the object becomes "it" and presents another mystery object. This continues until all students have a turn.

Teacher-to-Teacher

I usually schedule this activity in two half-hour sessions rather than one long one. The shorter sessions keep the interest level high.

If students are having difficulty identifying a mystery object, I will ask them specific questions about its properties to help with the identification. The vocabulary list is also an important resource for writing an accurate description.

....

MAROONED

Focus

In this show and tell style of speech, students practice oral composition.

Grade Levels: 3–8

Purpose

This activity has always been a favorite with my students because it allows them to reveal their personal interests during a short speech presentation to the class. The speech format has a simple structure, yet it allows students to practice speaking in front of an audience. During the speech, the "objects" that are shown help to prop up the speaker's confidence. Attention is focused on the props rather than on the speaker.

Benefits
- develops confidence in front of an audience
- builds organizational skills
- improves knowledge of self
- strengthens communication skills

Materials Needed
- Each student brings a bag (for example, a brown paper bag) with three objects or symbols of the objects inside (for example: a book, a pen, a diary).

Description of the Activity

Session 1 (Directions and Modeling)

I direct students to prepare a bag with three objects or symbols of objects (usually a homework assignment). I might say the following: "These objects are things that you would want to have with you if you were marooned on a deserted island. You should assume that your basic needs for survival are met, so none of the three objects should be needed for survival. Each of you will be showing your objects, one by one. As you pull out each object from your bag, explain to your audience why you chose to take that object along. Present your objects in a logical order. Begin your speech with a short introductory sentence (for example: 'If I were marooned on a deserted island, I would bring these three objects.'). After you explain why you chose each of the objects, end the speech with a closing sentence."

I then model the activity by showing my paper bag and the objects in it. Following my demonstration, I hand out written directions for the assignment and tell the students to prepare their speech following the directions given.

Session 2 (The Presentations)

The class gathers in our meeting area and each student comes equipped with the brown paper bag with the objects concealed inside. I ask for a volunteer to start. At this point I encourage the kids to speak extemporaneously as they remove their objects one by one from the bag. A few might choose to read their speech, but most I find are confident enough to make their presentation without it.

Teacher-to-Teacher

After I give the directions for this activity, the kids often ask me, "What if my object won't fit in the bag?" I tell them to draw the object, label it, and put the drawing in the bag.

For students who feel uncomfortable speaking extemporaneously, I suggest that they use index cards. Each card has the name of the object and the reason why the object is in the brown bag. They can read the card while they show the object to the group. When I have a large class, I divide the presentations into two sessions.

3 Games and Activities to Enhance Language Learning

The thirteen lessons in this chapter touch upon a variety of topics in writing, listening, and speaking. Many of the lessons are taught through *game playing*. Other lessons incorporate the strategies of *pantomime* and *choral reading*. Importantly, all the lessons can be accomplished in one teaching session of an hour or less and do not need extensive preparation by the teacher.

Three lessons teach the recognition of parts of speech ("Add an Adjective or Adverb," "Mime a Verb," and "Word Operation") through games. Other all-class games are designed to build vocabulary and spelling skills. They are "Minefield," "Spell It!" and "Mystery Words." The objective of the lessons called "Sentence Building" and "Punctuation Pantomime" is to teach grammar and punctuation.

Some of the lessons combine writing and performance. In "Simple Action Pantomime," for example, the students prepare a sequential list of actions needed to perform a routine activity. After the writing, they each present their pantomime for the class. In "Fractured Nursery Rhymes," which teaches rhyming patterns and meter in poetry, the learners work in groups to rewrite ("fracture") familiar nursery rhymes and then perform them. The focus of "Writing Around" is on creating dialogue for a script.

Although all the lessons strengthen oral language and listening skills, there are two in particular that concentrate on these areas. In "Rhyme Time," the students participate in a choral reading of nursery rhymes to practice clear speech and develop performance techniques. The focus of "Participation Stories" is on the development of listening and predicting skills. The audience joins in during a read-aloud story with simple actions, repeated phrases, and sound effects as they interact with the teacher.

··

ADD AN ADJECTIVE OR ADVERB

Focus

Played in small groups, this game develops an awareness of descriptive detail in writing.

Grade Levels: 3–8

Purpose

Young writers typically focus on telling the reader what's happening, frequently listing actions. They neglect the descriptive detail that helps the reader create a picture in the mind's eye. This game helps writers develop an awareness of the need for descriptive detail.

Benefits

- improves concentration
- increases descriptive vocabulary, especially sensory detail
- sharpens active listening skills
- helps with recognition of adjectives and adverbs as parts of speech

Materials Needed

- index cards with core sentences (sentences without descriptive detail) printed on each

Description of the Activity

I divide the students into groups of five or six players. I give the leader of each group index cards that have simple "core" sentences printed on them. The leader starts the game by reading a "core" sentence (Example: The dog ran out of the house.). The next player to the leader's right repeats the sentence and adds one descriptive word. The second player to the right repeats the sentence again using the new word that was added and then adds another descriptive word. The game continues around the circle until the last player adds a word and the newly embellished sentence is completed. After this, the leader states a new "core" sentence. The game might be played like this:

- The leader: The dog ran out of the house.
- Player 1: The *big* dog ran out of the house.
- Player 2: The big *shaggy* dog ran out of the house.
- Player 3: The big shaggy dog ran *quickly* out of the house.
- Player 4: The big shaggy dog ran quickly out of the *white* house.
- Player 5: The big shaggy dog ran quickly out of the white *shingled* house.
- Player 6: The big shaggy dog ran quickly out of the *dilapidated* white shingled house.

(*Note:* A variation of the game is played in one large circle and cards are passed out to every sixth or seventh player to start a new sentence.)

Teacher-to-Teacher

After the students have played the game several times, they are ready for independent work. I give them a short printed paragraph and have them rewrite it, adding descriptive detail. It's fun to share all the different solutions that the writers create. I caution them, however, that a good piece of writing is not necessarily one that is packed with adjectives or adverbs. This game is simply to develop an *awareness* that descriptive detail helps to *show* rather than *tell* the reader the story.

··

MIME-A-VERB

Focus

The focus is on the recognition of verbs and rhyming words.

Grade Levels: 4–8

Purpose

In this activity, the kids have some fun while learning about *verbs*. Working in teams, they brainstorm for solutions, pantomime their answers, and in the process they expand their verb vocabulary.

Benefits
- promotes an understanding of the function of a verb
- reviews the usage of rhyming words

- increases vocabulary
- provides an opportunity to use collaboration skills

Materials Needed
- index cards with rhyming verbs (example: crawl-fall-call-haul) printed on each (Examples are in the Teacher-to-Teacher section at the end of this lesson.)

Description of the Activity

I organize two teams of about six students. One team becomes "it" and they are sent out of the room. The other team is given an index card with rhyming words (example: crawl-fall-call-haul). From the list of words, they pick *one verb that is the actual answer* (for example, haul); and they pick *one verb that rhymes with the answer* (for example, crawl). This is the word they give to the other team when they return.

I call the "it" team back into the room and they say, "What is your verb?" The other team responds, "Our verb is crawl." At this point, members of the "it" team consult each other to guess the rhyming verb that they think is actually the correct one (it will be a word that rhymes with "crawl"). When an agreement is made, they *pantomime the verb*. If it is the correct answer, the other team applauds. If it is incorrect, the "it" team confers again and comes up with another word to pantomime. The guessing continues until the team finds the solution. If the team gives up, they go out of the room once again and a new round begins. However, if the "it" group guesses the correct answer, then a new team of six goes out of the room and another team of six is chosen to pick a verb that will challenge the new players. (See Figure 3–1.)

Teacher-to-Teacher

Students who have mastered verbs as a part of speech have no difficulty playing "Mime a Verb." Using the index cards is one way to ensure that the verbs chosen are ones that can be dramatized and are words that are familiar to the students. Examples of rhyming verbs to be printed on index cards are the following:

- trace-embrace-lace-place
- pack-quack-smack-whack-attack
- crawl-fall-call-haul
- play-sway-weigh-spray
- peek-shriek-sneak-speak-seek

Figure 3–1   Students mime a verb for the audience

- sneeze-squeeze-seize-freeze
- feed-freed-lead
- cheer-smear-sneer-spear
- sell-smell-yell-fell-spell
- chew-flew-threw-glue
- hide-ride-slide-guide-divide
- wink-drink-shrink-stink
- whip-skip-drip-slip-trip
- knit-quit-split-sit
- drop-hop-chop-mop-shop
- tow-throw-row-sew-stow-tiptoe
- lick-pick-flick-kick
- stroll-roll-poll-bowl
- mold-scold-blindfold-sold
- poke-smoke-woke-broke
- hurt-squirt-flirt-spurt
- beat-cheat-greet-heat-meet-eat

- gave-crave-rave-save-shave-wave
- stare-glare-share-pair-scare-wear
- bring-fling-sing-cling-swing-ring

••

WORD OPERATION

Focus

This game provides practice identifying parts of speech.

Grade Levels: 3–6

Purpose

Throughout the intermediate and middle grades, students are introduced to parts of speech during grammar lessons. Even after the lessons are taught and retaught, it can be challenging for kids to remember the names and functions of each part of speech. Constant review and practice are needed. This game, which is loosely modeled after a children's game called "Operation," provides practice identifying parts of speech in an interesting and relaxed way.

Benefits
- reviews parts of speech
- reviews the functions of the parts of speech

Materials Needed
- tongs (the style used in the kitchen or for the barbecue) to simulate the "forceps"
- ten sentences that have a variety of examples using parts of speech (Print the sentences with only a single word on each index card, so in the following example there would be seven cards.)

    Example: The shaggy dog scooted across the field. On one side of the card is a word from the sentence (for example, "shaggy") and on the other side of the card is the part of speech (for example, "adjective").
- an outline of a human body on newsprint (Trace a volunteer with a black magic marker.)
- a chart listing parts of speech with short definitions next to each

Description of the Activity

I direct students to sit in a semicircle, similar to an arrangement for a read-aloud session. At one end of the circle, I position my easel. On chart paper, the parts of speech are listed (noun, pronoun, verb, adverb, adjective, preposition, article) with a short definition next to each. I tell students that they are all "doctors" who are about to perform "operations." The "patients" are the sentences that will be placed on the "operating table" (inside the outline of the body).

When the "chief surgeon" (the teacher or any student who might be a suitable leader) announces the part that needs to be removed during the "operation," the appointed "doctor" needs to grab the "forceps" (tongs) and remove the part (the word on the index card). The "chief surgeon" might say, "Dr. Sarah, would you please operate on the patient ('The shaggy dog scooted across the field') to remove the adjective." The student then picks up the "forceps" and grabs the card with the word "shaggy" on it. The "chief surgeon" might direct that one or two more parts be removed from the "patient" before moving on to the next "patient" (another sentence). If the student removes the wrong part from the "patient," then a second doctor is appointed to assist in redoing the "operation" in order to save the "patient."

Teacher-to-Teacher

I try to give everyone a turn during this game. Students are anxious to be the "doctor" who "operates" successfully. For students who are challenged by the concept of speech parts, I partner them with a student who understands the idea. The "chief surgeon" may give hints in the form of questions to move the game along. We sometimes use sound effects. If a patient is in danger (the wrong part is about to be extracted), there might be a "beep-beep-beep-beep" sound to indicate danger.

••

MINEFIELD

Focus

The lesson focuses on vocabulary development.

Grade Levels: 3–8

Purpose

This game is a favorite with my students. It's easy to learn and gives the kids practice using directional words (for example: forward, backward, diagonally, left, right, up, down, front, back, beside, in between, etc.). It also encourages the use of words that describe a quality of movement (for example: slowly, carefully, on tiptoe, smoothly, with baby steps, etc.).

Benefits

- strengthens listening skills
- develops the use of directional vocabulary
- improves cooperation and group trust

Materials Needed

- a variety of soft objects that will not injure the players if they are stepped on during the game (for example: scarves, chalkboard eraser, magazines, writing paper, soft hats, newspaper, beanbag, etc.)

Description of the Activity

The students sit in a circle in an open area of the classroom. Inside the circle, I scatter a variety of objects, covering much of the space evenly. I choose someone to be "it" and put a blindfold on that player. Then I choose two "navigators" who will give a series of verbal directions to the blindfolded player to help "it" successfully cross the "minefield" without stepping on a "mine." After turning the blindfolded player around a few times, the journey from one side of the circle to the opposite side begins as the navigators call out directions. Taking turns, the navigators might sound something like this:

> Take four baby steps forward and stop. Lift up your left foot and take a giant step out to the left and slide your right foot to meet your left. Walk straight ahead four paces. Turn a quarter turn to your right. Take two steps forward. Lift your right knee high, stretch out your leg and take a giant step forward, then bring your left foot next to your right.

I watch for any contact in the "minefield" and if "it" touches an object, I shout "contact!" and the players in the circle make the sound effect for an explosion. When the player is out, the leader chooses another student to be blindfolded along with two new navigators.

Teacher-to-Teacher

After practicing this game, the players become quite adept at choosing the specific directional words that are needed to help "it" safely travel across the "minefield." Once students have played the game, they beg to play it every day. (*Note:* If there is sensitivity to the idea of a "minefield," the game can be changed to "navigating an airplane" or any other idea that seems appropriate for your class.)

....

SPELL IT!

Focus

This game is a stimulating way to practice weekly spelling words.

Grade Levels: 3–6

Purpose

I'm always trying new ways to interest my kids in developing their vocabularies. I use this game to practice the weekly lists with the class. The word lists are generated from words that I frequently see misspelled in their writing, or words that they need for lessons in reading, science, math, or social studies.

Benefits

- provides visual and tactile practice for spelling words
- encourages group teamwork

Materials Needed

- three sets of alphabet cards on 5 × 8 index cards or paper (I make one set on the computer, then photocopy as many as I need and laminate them); a set includes two copies of each consonant and three copies of each vowel

Description of the Activity

I divide the class into three teams with eight or more players on each team. The teams sit together at desks or tables. Each team receives one set of alphabet cards that are distributed among the players. Players are responsible for organizing their letters into piles ready to grab as needed to spell a word. I then remind students of the rules of the game, "When I call out a word, find the letter cards that spell the word. If a team thinks it has the correct spelling for the word, then the team *stands up* in a line showing the cards in front to spell out the word. The team that stands up first with the correct spelling of the word gets one point. Remember the *whispers only* rule while you work to spell the word."

Teacher-to-Teacher

When I play this game at the start of the school year, I leave the spelling list posted while we play. The focus then is on team coordination and on practicing the spelling of a word. After the learners have played the game during several sessions, I take down the list and they spell from memory.

When I organize my teams, I make sure that there is a mixture of students who are good spellers along with those who are not. The team approach in this game benefits the students who are challenged by spelling.

....

MYSTERY WORDS

Focus

This lesson focuses on dictionary skills and vocabulary development.

Grade Levels: 4–8

Purpose

I use this game toward the end of the school year to provide a change of pace from normal spelling lesson routines. It has some similarities to the parlor game called "Balderdash." Players use many skills to participate in this game. Using the dictionary, writing, reading, speaking, acting, and collaboration are all involved in "Mystery Words."

Benefits
- enhances descriptive writing skills
- provides an opportunity to practice using a dictionary
- strengthens speaking skills and reading fluency
- builds collaborative work skills

Materials Needed
- dictionaries
- large index cards

Description of the Activity

Session 1 (Preparation)
Depending on the size of my class, I divide the students into groups of about three to four players. Students work with dictionaries to find words that are unfamiliar to classmates (I suggest words that have simple definitions).

Groups are given a stack of large index cards. Each individual in the group needs to find at least three "Mystery Words." When a word is located, the student prints the word and the definition on the card. Following that, the player creates three fake definitions for the same word each on a separate index card (the number of fake definitions depends on the number of kids on each team).

Group members should help each other create clever, believable fake definitions. (*Note:* The dictionary work could also be an individual homework assignment.) While the kids are working, I circulate from group to group to confer with the writers. I encourage the selection of appropriate words and assist them with the creation of fake definitions. When the groups have completed their work, they clip the index cards, one pile for each of the "Mystery Words."

Session 2 (the Game)

To prepare, we set up the classroom by moving desks to create two tables facing each other (each long enough to hold one of the groups). I divide the groups into two large teams (for example, if I have six groups of four students, I put three groups on one side and three groups on the other side to create two large teams, twelve on Team A and twelve on Team B). One group of four from Team A sits at one table and one group of four from Team B sits at the other table. "Mystery Word" is now ready to start.

If Team A is up first, a mystery word is selected to stump the other team (B). Each player on Team A takes a turn saying the mystery word and reading the definition (real or fake) from the index card while trying to convince the opposing team that the definition for the word is the *real* one (here's where acting skills are important). The group from Team B confers and votes on which one they think is the *real* definition. If Team B guesses correctly, they earn a point for their team, and if they guess incorrectly, Team A earns a point for fooling them.

In the next round, Team B leads off by selecting a mystery word and each member of the group reads a definition, trying to mislead the other team. Team A makes the guess. In the following round, two new groups go up to play (frequent group changes keep it interesting for all the kids). After these groups each have a turn, a switch is made again until every group has had at least one turn. At this point, the rotation begins again with the first two groups. The game continues until teams run out of mystery words or out of time.

Teacher-to-Teacher

My kids love this game and will spend hours creating fake definitions to fool the opposing team. To keep the game fair, I don't allow coaching from other team members who are not sitting at the table playing a round.

In a variation of the game that is suitable for young players, the *teacher* creates lists of "Mystery Words" and passes them out to the groups. The students in each group look up the definitions and create fake definitions for each word. The game then proceeds as described previously.

•••

SENTENCE BUILDING

Focus

The focus is on creating complete sentences with punctuation.

Grade Levels: 3–6

Purpose

I find this drama game especially useful in the intermediate grades or with any students who are unsure of end punctuation. It helps learners understand how to construct a sentence as the group forms them collectively and uses appropriate punctuation.

Benefits

- sharpens listening skills
- develops an awareness of group interaction
- provides practice constructing sentences
- strengthens end punctuation skills

Materials Needed: None

Description of the Activity

The children sit in a circle in our open space. I explain to the group that they will form sentences with each player contributing *one word*. I usually start by saying the first word, then the player to my right adds a second, then the next player on the right adds a third, and so on until the sentence ends with a period or any suitable end punctuation. I usually suggest a topic focus—for example, a field trip, the lunchroom, activities at recess, spelling words, and so forth. This way, when one sentence ends, another sentence immediately begins and the sentence building continues around the circle until I call a halt. One sentence might look like this:

Player 1: The	Player 2: monkey	Player 3: at
Player 4: the	Player 5: zoo	Player 6: ate
Player 7: a	Player 8: banana	Player 9: period

Teacher-to-Teacher

I find that older players use more complicated sentence construction and punctuation. We add commas and quotations. I caution players about run-on sentences and the need for clarity.

As the group develops skill with this activity, entire stories can be created. Instead of one word, each player contributes one sentence and it continues going around the circle until the story is completed.

PUNCTUATION PANTOMIME

Focus

The lesson provides kinesthetic practice for punctuation usage.

Grade Levels: 3–5

Purpose

I use this game at the start of the year to review end punctuation and I continue to use it throughout the year to practice new punctuation skills that I've taught in my mini-lessons. Once the kids learn the motions that show each punctuation mark, they perform them easily without hesitation. By practicing the use of punctuation kinesthetically, they are more likely to remember how to use these marks and understand why they are needed to help the reader make sense of written words.

Benefits

- strengthens recognition and usage of punctuation marks
- improves listening skills
- increases group cooperation

Materials Needed

- a chart listing a series of unpunctuated sentences or sentences on flash cards that can be posted one at a time
- a chart showing the hand motions for each punctuation mark

Description of the Activity

The students gather in the open area of our classroom in lines facing me. I first teach them the pantomime motions that show punctuation marks. They are as follows:

- period: right hand is thrust forward in front of the body in a stop motion (like a traffic cop)
- question mark: right arm is curved in a half circle above the head and the left hand is fisted in front of the waist
- exclamation point: both arms reach above the head, palms together while jumping once (this emphasizes that it's meant to be said in excitement)
- comma: right arm curved in a half circle *in front* of the body
- quotation marks: use the index and middle fingers in a quick up and down motion of either the right or left hand
- semicolon: make the same motion as the comma (right arm curved in a half circle in front of the body) and add a fist above it with the left hand
- apostrophe: right arm is curved in a half circle *above* the head
- colon: right and left hands are fisted, one on top of the other, at waist level

After we've practiced the motions a few times, we are ready to begin. I leave a chart with pictures of each position posted in front. Mastery of the motions is not needed because the students will gradually learn them as we play the game. To start, I post sentences that are already punctuated. As a group we rehearse saying the sentence and making the motions for the marks. I perform along with the students to model the idea. An example would be as follows:

Posted sentence: Mary, where are you going?

Student response: "Mary (comma motion) where are you going (question mark motion)"

After students practice a few examples, they are ready to try sentences that have the punctuation left out. I keep my examples simple for the first few lessons. I limit punctuation to *one or two marks* only. As the year goes on, I make them more complicated. A posted sentence might look like this:

Posted Sentence: Stop the fighting yelled the coach

Student Response: (Quotation mark motion) Stop the fighting (exclamation mark motion followed by the quotation mark motion) yelled the coach (period motion)

Teacher-to-Teacher

A variation of this game is to divide the class into groups of four to five students. Each group is given a sentence to rehearse for a few minutes. When they have determined the correct punctuation, they perform their "Punctuation Pantomime" for the rest of the class. If a group has incorrectly left out a mark or misused a mark, then I help them determine the correct marks and they perform again for the class.

....

SIMPLE ACTION PANTOMIME

Focus

The focus is on using sequential order in writing.

Grade Levels: 3–8

Purpose

This pantomime activity develops an awareness of sequential order in writing. Writing in a logical order requires the use of order words such as *then, next,* and also directional words such as *up, down, right, left.* When students report their observations in a science experiment or explain how they solved a math problem, I find that the writing sometimes lacks logical sequencing. This pantomime activity addresses that problem.

Benefits
- gives the learners practice using sequencing in writing
- strengthens the use of directional words and specific action verbs
- sharpens perception and concentration
- develops confidence in front of an audience

Materials Needed
- a sample sequential list of a simple action

Description of the Activity

A day or two before we perform the pantomimes, I model the activity in our open meeting area. I direct students to watch as I perform a simple pantomime, telling them to carefully note the sequence of my movements and be ready to name the action that was being mimed. I pick a simple everyday action such as "brushing teeth." When the mime is completed, the students name the activity and recall the various actions in the mime.

Afterwards, I show them my detailed sequential list of all the actions that I used during the pantomime of brushing my teeth (see the model at the end of this lesson). The list of about thirty actions might start something like this:

- *Open* the right hand drawer of the cabinet with the *right* hand.
- *Remove* a tube of toothpaste from the drawer with the *right* hand.
- *Place* the tube on the *right* side of the counter.
- *Close* the drawer with the *right* hand.
- *Pick up* the toothbrush from the holder with the *right* hand.

After students look at my sequence of actions, I ask them, "What do you notice about the words that were used to describe the actions?" Students instantly pick out the directional words: up, down, right, left, and so forth. Then they notice that each sentence begins with a verb: remove, pick up, flick, squeeze, flip, and so forth. I tell students that they will each be performing a simple action pantomime and direct them to pick an action, write each step in sequence, and practice the pantomime. This can be assigned for homework.

The next day, we meet in our open space and each student comes with the sequential steps listed for the action. One by one, they each perform the pantomime while the audience is directed to note the detailed steps and to name the action when the scene is finished.

Teacher-to-Teacher

To help my kids choose an appropriate action, I show a list of suggestions that are familiar to children. Here are a few examples: pack a school backpack, make a bed, wash your hands, make a sandwich, feed the dog or cat, put on a coat, wrap a present, put on sunscreen lotion at the beach, dry yourself with a towel at the beach or pool, comb or brush your hair. The attention to detail usually produces excellent pantomimes, sometimes remarkable for young kids who are inexperienced in mime.

As a follow-up to this activity, I lead a discussion about feelings by asking students: "How do feelings influence your actions? For example, if I was very sad when I brushed my teeth, how might my actions change? Suppose you were very angry with your parents when you packed your backpack, how would the action look then?" I then ask students to think of a feeling or a mood and repeat the "Simple Action Pantomime" adding a *feeling* or *mood* to the scene.

Sample Pantomime, "Brushing My Teeth"

- Open right drawer of cabinet with the right hand.
- Remove tube of toothpaste from drawer with the right hand.
- Place the tube on the right side of the counter.
- Pick up the toothbrush from the holder with the right hand.
- Flick the faucet handle up with the left hand.
- Run the brush under the water.
- Push the faucet handle back down with the left hand.
- Pick up the tube of toothpaste with the left hand from the right side of the counter.
- Flip open the cap with the left thumb.
- Squeeze the toothpaste onto the brush.
- Flip the cap back on with the left index finger.
- Cross the left hand in front of the body and place the tube on the right side of the counter.
- Rest the left hand on the left hip near the waist.
- Brush the front teeth with an up and down motion with the right hand.
- Brush the left side with an up and down motion.
- Brush the right side with an up and down motion.
- Flick the brush with a twisting wrist motion on the bottom left teeth.
- Flick the brush with a twisting wrist motion on the bottom right teeth.
- Repeat the same action first on the upper left, then on the upper right.
- Flip open the faucet with the left hand.
- Rinse the brush with the right hand.
- Close the tap with the left hand.

- Tap the brush on the edge of the sink.
- Replace the brush in the holder with the right hand.
- Reach for the cup on the left side of the sink with the right hand.
- Flick open the faucet with the left hand and fill the cup.
- Close the faucet with the left hand.
- Rinse mouth, spit in sink.
- Put down the cup with the right hand.

••

FRACTURED NURSERY RHYMES

Focus

The focus is on creating and sharing poetry in a performance reading.

Grade Levels: 3–6

Purpose

In the primary grades, children are introduced to the music of language. They sing and act out songs, recite nursery rhymes, and experience literature with rhyme and rhythm patterns (for example, Dr. Seuss books). By the intermediate grades, these experiences are often not a part of learning. This lesson is a way to remind students that poetry can be fun to read, say, and write. It's an activity that I use early in the year to create an interest in poetry and to overcome their fears of writing in this genre. Later in the year, I introduce other styles of poetry. By then students are primed to write more challenging forms of verse.

Benefits
- creates an interest in poetry
- develops confidence in the genre
- provides experience with counting the meter and identifying rhyme scheme patterns
- presents an opportunity to work collaboratively
- enhances oral language skills during the presentation

Materials Needed

- Mother Goose nursery rhymes
- rhyming dictionaries (optional)
- one transparency with a nursery rhyme

Description of the Activity

I start this activity with a mini-lesson. I read several nursery rhymes asking students to listen to the sounds in the poem. The students notice that each verse has a rhythm and a rhyme. I post one nursery rhyme on the overhead projector and ask students to identify the words that rhyme. After the learners come up and underline the rhyming words, we identify the pattern of rhyming words in a line and code the lines that rhyme (for example, an a-b-a-b pattern).

Next I question them about the rhythm. We clap out the beats in each word or tap with a finger on the desk. I mark a beat stroke on the transparency above each syllable to make it easier to count. Again the kids notice the pattern (for example, a meter line pattern might be: 7 beats, 6 beats, 7 beats, 6 beats).

Following that, I distribute a new nursery rhyme, the same one to each student and direct them to find the number of beats in each line and the rhyming pattern. I work the room helping those who need it and then we discuss the results together. If most of the students are successful then I move on to the writing of the "Fractured Nursery Rhymes."

I begin by writing a poem with the entire class to model the idea of writing a "Fractured Nursery Rhyme." We start with a familiar rhyme and "fracture" it by changing words to make it a new rhyme. Here are a couple of the fractured rhymes that the class wrote with me (the students contributing a word or a line):

Example 1:

Mary had a little frog
His skin was slimy green
Everywhere that Mary jogged
The slimy frog was seen

Example 2:

Peter Peter pancake eater
Had a dog and couldn't keep her
Put her in a nice hotel
There she lived life very well

At this point, students are ready to write with a partner or a three-some to create their own verse. I distribute nursery rhymes on a handout and books of nursery rhymes are located on every table. Students pick one rhyme that they are eager to "fracture" and work to rewrite it. Rhyming dictionaries are available for reference as needed. I set a time limit and to facilitate the process, I roam from group to group to check on progress and assist with finding the appropriate rhyming word and determine meter or the rhyming pattern. After the poets complete the fractured rhymes, they prepare for a class performance. I remind them to think about articulation, pronunciation, projection, and inflection (see "Rhyme Time" in this chapter). Groups take turns presenting their "Fractured Nursery Rhyme."

Teacher-to-Teacher

Modeling the idea of how to "fracture" a nursery rhyme is an important step in the process. Students need to practice finding the meter and the rhyme pattern. Rhyming dictionaries are also an excellent resource for this lesson.

....

WRITING AROUND

Focus

This collaborative game focuses on writing dialogue.

Grade Levels: 4–8

Purpose

During this group writing activity, the kids benefit from the creative thinking of other group members. It relaxes students during the drafting process as they create dialogue in response to another character, which is similar to improvised dialogue during a drama session. I use this activity as an introduction to playwriting because it familiarizes students with the format used for dialogue and stage directions.

Benefits
- introduces the format for playwriting
- develops playwriting skills
- encourages collaboration as students support and build on the contributions of others
- strengthens the confidence of the writers

Materials Needed

- pencil and paper for each student
- index cards with a different scene prompt for each group of three to four students

Example:

Where: An orphanage late at night
Who: Miss Parker (the director), Mary (an orphan), Mabel (an orphan)
What (the problem): An orphan is missing
Opening Line
Mary: Hey! Where's Mindy? She's not in her bed!

Description of the Activity

I organize groups of three or four students and pass out the scene prompt cards to each group. One writer copies the first line of the scene onto the paper. On completion, a second writer adds another line, then passes the paper and a third writer adds a new line to the script. The collaborative effort should be emphasized, with each student contributing lines for a character (an alternative method is to have one student act as the recorder as each contributes a line). During each swap, a new line is added to the script. New characters may be created also, but I caution them to limit the additions to one or two. I suggest that the writers take the time to reread the script before they add a line. Lines need to develop logically from the beginning through to the middle and finally to the end (the solution to the problem). If necessary, stage directions may be included in parentheses.

The time limit for this activity is determined by watching the students as they write. When I sense that students are finishing (usually about twenty to thirty minutes), I ask them to reread the script and make any needed revisions. At the end of the lesson, each group performs the scene (Readers Theatre style) for the rest of the class.

Teacher-to-Teacher

The results of this activity are sometimes astonishingly good and at times they are silly. Nevertheless, the kids always seem like they are relaxed and having fun. In the end, they've overcome any fears they may have had about scriptwriting, and usually beg for another session to add a scene or elaborate on the completed one. Ultimately, they've all learned how to use a script format, and develop a scene with a beginning, middle, and end.

If there are enough computers in the classroom, I organize the groups around a computer. One student types while the others contribute lines. At the end, it's possible to print three scripts, which eliminates having to share one script during the Readers Theatre.

....

RHYME TIME

Focus

This choral reading activity is an opportunity to practice clear speech.

Grade Levels: 3–5

Purpose

I use this lesson to help children become more aware of their speech. I make no attempt to judge the way they speak because each child has a manner of speaking that is expressive of his or her environment and personality. However, it is important that children learn how to best communicate their thoughts clearly. This lesson provides practice to help students make some adjustments in their speech.

Benefits
- provides practice with articulation, pronunciation, and projection
- promotes an understanding of rhyming patterns and rhythms
- strengthens read-aloud skills
- allows for experimentation using variety in the rate, the volume, and the word emphasis

Materials Needed
- a book of nursery rhymes
- photocopied selections of nursery rhymes

Description of the Activity

I gather students in our open area to present a Mother Goose nursery rhyme book. I read several of the rhymes for enjoyment, emphasizing clear pronunciation and articulation as I read them. Afterwards, I pick one to practice with the entire class, posting it for all to read. The first reading is done in "echo" fashion. I read a line and the learners repeat the line. I challenge students to mimic my articulation and pronunciation as closely as possible. After we finish, I make a few suggestions, such as: "When we practice again, I need to hear the *t*'s better. Try to open your mouth wider when you speak." During the next reading, we take turns. I say one line and the entire class says the next line.

Once confidence with the reading is established, I divide the class into smaller groups, assigning lines to each group or sometimes to an individual who might say a line, a phrase, or a single word. Through questioning, I encourage students to think about tips for a successful choral reading (for example, pronunciation, articulation, word emphasis, and projection). We perform it again.

Later in the session (or the following lesson), I divide the class into groups and allow each group to choose (or I assign) a nursery rhyme from the photocopied selections. Each group prepares a choral reading to present to the rest of the class. This time, I add another challenge by suggesting they also think about using variety in volume, rate of speed, and emphasis. I demonstrate what this means by posting one sentence and reading it in a variety of ways, then the students join in with me. I also suggest that they create a few gestures or actions that would be appropriate when they perform the rhyme. The groups practice and then present their work for the others in the drama circle.

Teacher-to-Teacher

I frequently give a viewing purpose to the audience. In this activity, I ask the audience to make note of performance strategies that were especially effective. I lead a postperformance discussion on this topic. I also ask each group to reflect on what worked well and what could be improved if they repeated the performance. If there is extra time, I ask students to repeat the performance and include their revisions.

Although we usually associate nursery rhymes with young children, I find that they are appropriate with any age group. Whenever I use picture books or material that might appear "babyish" to my kids, I explain to them why I am using that particular resource, and they relax and accept it as part of the learning experience.

· ·

PARTICIPATION STORIES

Focus

The learners respond orally and physically to a read-aloud story.

Grade Levels: 3–5

Purpose

"Participation Theatre" is a popular form of children's theatre. The audience joins in during the performance with chants, pantomime, sound effects, improvisation, clapping, singing, and so forth. This lesson encourages participation in a read-aloud session modeled after Participation

Theatre. In some ways it is similar to an interactive read-aloud in which the teacher stops to ask questions, interject ideas, and ask the listeners their personal thoughts. However, "Participation Stories" focuses more on a physical and oral response that involves creative problem solving.

A read-aloud is an opportunity for me to model fluency, correct pronunciation, articulation, phrasing, and variety in inflection. I change my voice for each character. My facial expressions are animated and enthusiastic. Gestures and props are incorporated to enhance the drama of the event. To create a mood, I vary the volume of my voice from soft to loud and the pacing from slow to fast. Occasionally, I use a costume piece. In other words, as I read, I use my acting skills to dramatize the story.

Benefits

- increases comprehension of the characters, plot, and setting
- improves vocal expression
- enhances listening and predicting skills
- develops problem-solving skills
- motivates independent reading

Materials Needed

- an appropriate story that has an exciting plot, engaging characters, colorful dialogue, and provides opportunities for participation (See a list of suggestions at the end of this lesson.)
- various objects to create sound effects (optional)

Description of the Activity

I introduce the story by showing the cover of the book and giving the students a listening purpose. For example, I might say, "Listen to the dialogue in the story. Ask yourself, what does the dialogue reveal about the personality of the characters?" The listening purpose is determined by the participation activity that I've planned for the students. Some participation might occur *during* the read-aloud and other participation might take place *after* the reading. Participation responses could be one of the following:

- Make sound effects at the appropriate time.
- Say a line(s) that is repeated often in the story or poem.
- Join in to insert a word or complete a sentence (cloze technique).
- Create facial or hand gestures that fit the plot line.
- Sing a song appropriate for the text.
- Recite a chant.

- Pantomime actions in the story, or mime emotions of the characters.
- Create a line in response to a character.
- Create a new line that the character might say in the book.
- Respond in role as a character from the book in a new situation.
- Create tableaux of the major plot events of the story.
- Pantomime the plot actions of the story as the teacher narrates.
- Improvise dialogue based on what is known about the character and plot events.

Teacher-to-Teacher

There are many books suitable for dramatic reading. Entire books and extensive lists have been created to help teachers select quality literature. Many folk tales, fairy tales, and narrative poems present opportunities for participation. As a teacher, I feel that my most successful read-aloud books are those that I have personally selected based on my students' interests and needs, my needs, and the quality of the literature. First, I carefully read the book analyzing the characters. I pay attention to the dialogue and think about how I might portray a character's voice (like an actor might prepare for a role). I make notes of any words that need to be explained to the kids. I'm especially alert to any sections that might become possibilities for participation. I plan how I might extend the read-aloud experience into another lesson in writing or reading.

Although a read-aloud session is more typical in the primary grades, I find that older students still love it and truly look forward to our sessions. I feel that the read-aloud is one of the most effective strategies that I use in my teaching across the entire curriculum.

4 Activities to Promote an Understanding of Story Elements

The twelve lessons in this chapter are devoted to developing an understanding of the story elements of character, plot, setting, mood, and theme. They connect reading with writing through a variety of activities that use the following strategies: games, pantomime, tableau, improvisation, Readers Theatre, script reading, and interviewing.

There are five lessons devoted to *how writers reveal a character* to the reader. The topics are the following: dialogue to reveal character, physical traits of a character, character's emotion, and character's movement and gesture.

Four lessons concentrate on helping the learners understand *plot structure:* "On-the-Scene Reporter" and "Sticky Situations" call attention to conflict as a plot device. "Tableaux" and "You End It" teach the importance of rising action and the denouement.

"Exploring Setting" and "Mood Story" are lessons that are closely connected. They both explore the idea of *setting that shapes the action and the mood* of a story.

The final lesson focuses on the difficult concept of *theme* in a story. The lesson, "Theme Scene," combines a read-aloud book with improvisational drama to explore the idea of theme. Because teachers are less familiar with improvisation as a strategy, I carefully outline the steps of the process. Sample questions are provided to successfully guide students through the experience.

EXPLORING CHARACTERIZATION

Focus

The focus is on the use of dialogue as a device to reveal character traits.

Grade Levels: 3–5

Purpose

When I ask my students to describe a character that they have encountered in a piece of literature, they can usually come up with a few descriptive words. "He's mean," they might say. To help my kids make the connection between reading and writing, I want them to understand *how* they knew that the character was "mean." This activity emphasizes dialogue as a way to reveal character traits.

Benefits

- develops the understanding that writers use dialogue as a device to reveal a character
- provides an opportunity to practice listening skills
- provides an experience to read in the role of the book's character
- enhances reading fluency

Materials Needed

- chart paper
- cue cards with character lines printed on them
- a read-aloud book (*Hansel and Gretel* by James Marshall is used here)

Description of the Activity

I ask the learners to gather on the rug in the classroom (our open area). After showing them the cover of the book, I give a listening purpose. In this instance, I ask students to listen for the names of the characters in the book and think about what they say. I read *Hansel and Gretel* using dramatic voices for each character. After I finish the book, we discuss the listening purpose. I ask the listeners to tell me the names of the main characters and I record them on chart paper. Then I show a cue card with a line that was spoken by a character in the book. For example, the character of the wife says, "Those wretched children of yours are gobbling everything up. Do you want your pretty little wife to waste away?" I ask for volunteers to perform a dramatic reading of the lines of dialogue between the husband and wife. After the readings, I ask students to explain what this dialogue reveals about the wife. I record responses on the chart paper next to the character's name (for example: "mean," "selfish"). Then I show another cue card with a line spoken by another character. They take turns reading in dramatic voices. Then I follow it again with the question: What does this line reveal about Hansel? We do this for the all the main characters, accumulating a list of character traits next to each character's name.

At the closing of the lesson, I ask questions that promote a discussion of how they were able to understand something about the personality traits of each character in the book. (For example: How did the writer reveal the personality of the wife in the story? What techniques did the writer use?) Their responses indicate that they recognize that dialogue is a way for a writer to reveal something about the character. I then ask them to think about how they could use dialogue in their own writing.

Teacher-to-Teacher

Everyone usually wants a turn to give a dramatic reading. I make sure that I have multiple lines for each character printed on cue cards.

As a follow-up to this session, I assign students to work with a partner. They pick a scene from the book and write additional dialogue for the two characters. They take turns presenting the short scenes to the rest of the class in the drama circle. (*Note:* It's important to show students the format for writing dialogue.)

· ·

TELEPHONE CHAT

Focus

The lesson focuses on the literary device of revealing character traits through dialogue.

Grade Levels: 3–8

Purpose

I find this game particularly helpful to develop awareness in writers that dialogue can be used to reveal character traits to the reader. Young writers will often *tell* the reader something about the character rather than reveal the character through dialogue, action, and so forth. After the players achieve some skill with the telephone game, the conversations are more detailed, making clear *who* the characters are and *what* are their situations.

Benefits

- introduces the idea that a character can be revealed through dialogue
- provides an occasion to listen and respond in character
- presents an opportunity to practice problem-solving skills

Materials Needed

- two inactive telephones or cell phones are placed in the center of the circle.

Description of the Activity

The players sit in a circle. I walk around the outside and quietly tap one player on the shoulder. The player who was tapped reaches for a phone. Acting as the "operator," I give that player an identity (for example: "You are Mr. Smith, the principal of the school and you are calling Mrs. Mann about her daughter's behavior"). At this point, I make a telephone ringing sound and tap another student on the shoulder who immediately picks up the second phone and assumes the character that was suggested by the "operator." The players need to imagine that they are far away from each other. The conversation that the students improvise should solve the problem presented, that is, to reveal who their characters are through the dialogue. Examples of conversations might be:

- A student calls home to ask permission to go to the movies with a friend.
- A child calls his grandparent for his birthday.
- A neighbor calls next door to complain about the dog ruining the garden.
- A student calls another student to ask about homework.
- A student calls another student to organize a sleepover.

Teacher-to-Teacher

I encourage short conversations to keep everyone interested. Long conversations between two players can be an invitation for others to lose interest. Side-coaching is an important strategy for the teacher to use when the conversation slows. The questions that I ask guide the players and keep them focused during the interaction. I also ask questions to promote a discussion after each improvised conversation. (For example: "Were the identities of the characters revealed to us through the conversation? Tell me how.")

....

CAN YOU GIVE ME A DESCRIPTION?

Focus

The focus is on physical traits as a device to reveal a character.

Grade Levels: 3–5

Purpose

These games help the writer sharpen observational skills to develop characters in their writing. Physical traits are a good starting point because they are observable to the kids. Actors work hard to develop both the physical and emotional traits of the character being portrayed. They do this to make the character real for the audience. Writers do the same. To make a character come alive for the reader, physical and emotional detail is needed. Game 1 provides the oral rehearsal for Game 2, which is a pencil and paper task.

Benefits
- sharpens observational skills
- increases descriptive vocabulary
- develops an awareness of the importance of character description

Materials Needed
- Game 1: none
- Game 2: pencil and paper

Description of Game 1 (an Oral Activity)

I divide the class into groups of about four. When they are seated in their designated areas, I assign a simple task (for example, a question to discuss). After three or four minutes, I give a direction: "I will tap one person in each group on the shoulder. If I tap you, leave the group and sit somewhere in the room with your back to your group. No member of the group should be visible to you." At this point, I ask each person who has left the group to carefully describe one of the members of the group using details such as hair and eye color, hairstyle, shoes, clothes, and so forth. After the game is played once, the students know what to expect and become vigilant. For the next round, I shuffle the groups so that everyone is in a new group. I give the kids a few minutes to observe and then I call out the direction once again. The new students who are "it" must describe one person from the group in detail. Groups are reshuffled again and a new round begins.

Description of Game 2 (a Writing Activity)

In an open space in the classroom, I divide the class into two equal circles, one circle inside the other. If the groups are uneven, I join a group or ask a student to step out and assist me in leading the game. I give the following direction: "On my signal (I usually use a drum), begin to walk. The outside circle will walk in one direction (clockwise) and the inside circle will walk in the opposite direction (counterclockwise). When I bang the drum, stop and face the person next to you (similar to a mixer-style dance). That person is now your partner." When students have a partner I instruct them to head back to their desks, grab a paper and pencil (set out ahead of time), and sit with their partner. Each of the players writes a detailed physical description of his or her partner. When most students have completed the description, the partners share their work with each other.

Teacher-to-Teacher

These games raise an awareness of the need for character description. As a follow-up, I schedule several craft mini-lessons that examine how professional writers employ physical description and provide opportunities for my kids to practice this technique during writing time.

I've successfully used this activity in the intermediate grades and with college age students. In the middle grades there might be more sensitivity to physical descriptions, and I avoid using this activity. With the younger students, I make sure that I address the need for choosing descriptors that are not judgmental (for example, words like "fat" or "ugly" are hurtful to others).

....

MIME WITH EMOTION

Focus

This lesson develops an awareness of a character's emotion.

Grade Levels: 3–8

Purpose

Accomplished writers develop characters with strong feelings. Kids recognize the feelings of characters in a book, but their own stories portray characters more from the outside than the inside. When an actor prepares for a role, the inner emotions of the character being portrayed drive the physical behavior of the character. In this activity, the players experience many different emotions during the pantomimes, which raises their awareness of the need for emotion in the characters they develop in their stories.

Benefits

- develops an awareness of a range of possible emotions
- helps the learner recognize that inner emotion is often revealed through outward actions
- enhances concentration

Materials Needed

- A *list of suggestions* for pantomimes that are everyday actions familiar to your students (for example, packing a backpack, talking on the telephone, doing homework, tying shoes, combing hair, making a bed, washing dishes, feeding the dog or cat, drinking a glass of water, fixing a bowl of cereal, playing a computer game, waiting in the principal's office, reading a book)
- *Index cards with an emotion/feeling* printed on the card (for example, happy, sad, angry, fearful, excited, bored, aggressive, timid, frazzled, prudent, hateful, curious, proud)

Description of the Activity

I gather students in the open space of the classroom and divide them into groups of three or four. A group is sent into the playing area and given a suggestion for a pantomime (for example: packing your backpack). Students in the group each perform the pantomime in their own individual manner. I side-coach them with remarks such as: "Take your time." "Visualize the backpack." "See every item that goes into it." "Zip up every pocket."

When they finish, I ask the audience if they were able to "see" any of the items that went into the bags. After a short discussion, I pass out an index card to each student in the group that performed and give the following direction: "Look at the card, notice the emotion that is printed on the card, then return the card to me. You will now repeat the pantomime. This time, you need to add the feeling that was printed on your card." I challenge the audience: "Can you determine the emotion assigned to each player? How have the movement, gestures, and facial expressions changed?"

When the first group has finished, a new group takes their place up front and they are assigned an action for pantomime. When they finish, they repeat the mime, this time adding the emotion. The activity is repeated until all the groups have performed.

Teacher-to-Teacher

It is important that the audience watch the group of players carefully when emotions are added to notice how the performance changes physically. After a performance, I might single out a player to repeat the action while the audience makes a mental note of the body language. When the player finishes, I take chart paper and write the emotion at the top. Underneath I list all the gestures, movements, postures, and facial expressions that were noticed by the audience. These phrases (hunched shoulders, fisted hands, rapid walk, knitted brows, etc.) stimulate the students' thinking about utilizing physical description to reveal emotion in their own writing.

As a follow-up to this lesson, I post a nursery rhyme on chart paper (for example, "Little Miss Muffet"). I tell the students that we are going to read this poem in many different voices. I start by selecting a feeling, emotion, or mood (for example, "suspenseful"). I lead a reading of the poem in a suspenseful voice. After I have modeled the idea, I partner the students and assign a word to each couple. Here are a few choices that have worked well for me:

suspenseful	angrily	sadly	laughing voice	incredulously
tenderly	crisply	happily	nervously	snobbishly
tired	crying	sternly	seriously (like a news anchor)	

Couples find a spot in the room and take a few minutes to practice the rhymes using the feeling or mood assigned to them. The groups then take turns presenting their version of the nursery rhyme.

· ·

CHARACTER SLEUTHS

Focus

The lesson focuses on gesture as a device to describe a character.

Grade Levels: 3–8

Purpose

I want my writers to recognize the importance of characterization in their fiction writing. They are more likely to focus on outlining a detailed plot rather than developing a full-blown character. Teaching young writers specific strategies for character development helps them to sketch their characters more fully. This activity, which I call "Character Sleuths," develops an awareness of *gesture* as a strategy to reveal a character to the reader.

I experienced this activity myself in my first acting class and thought at the time that it was a productive exercise and fun as well. With that in mind, I tried it with my kids and they too enjoyed the experience.

Benefits
- enhances observation skills
- helps students recognize that gesture is a way to reveal a character's emotional state

Materials Needed
- pad and pencil

Description of the Activity

The preparation for this activity is done outside of class. I give my students the following direction: "You need to observe a person (hopefully unnoticed by that person) for about ten to fifteen minutes (or longer). Jot down the physical motions that you observe (for example: crossed arms, a tilt of the head, lips pressed together, pulling of the ear lobe, knitting of the brow, hands clasped, arms akimbo, crossing of the legs, etc.)." I go on to suggest some places where they might make their observations (for example: a cafeteria, a restaurant or fast food place, a library, a dentist's or doctor's waiting room, a bus, at home, a mall, etc.). When they have completed their observation, they need to practice imitating the gestures that they have noticed.

Note: I caution the sleuths not to reveal the name of the person (if it is known) that they are observing.

In the classroom, we gather in our open space and I lead off the activity with a few questions about their findings. They share some of their observations. Next, I organize groups of about three to four students. Each group is given a turn to present their characters using the gestures that they've observed. As each group is called up, I designate a setting (for example: a dentist's waiting room, a museum, a restaurant, a library, an airport waiting area, etc.). An example of the activity might be as follows:

Members of Group 1 who are told that they are in a *library* enter the imagined space and behave like their character. One student might be reading and *unconsciously twisting her hair*. Another student might be searching the shelves with his *hand on his chin*. A third student might be at a computer *bouncing his leg nervously*. A fourth student might be *rubbing her forehead* out of frustration as she tries to write a paper.

I assign the audience the task of noticing the gestures that are specific to each character. When the scene finishes, I ask the audience to share what they observed. Another group takes a turn in the performance area and I designate a new setting. This procedure continues until everyone has had a turn. By the end of the session, all the students are aware of gesture as a way to reveal a character's emotion.

Teacher-to-Teacher

I try to pick public places as settings for the scenes. In these places it is normal to have people who are strangers to each other in the same environment. The scenes are usually in pantomime, but occasionally, a few words emerge naturally as the actors interact in the chosen place.

As a follow-up to this lesson, I give a writing assignment. I direct my students to use the character that they have observed to *write a paragraph* employing the strategy of gesture to reveal the character. The following is an example of the writing assignment:

> Martin pressed his fingers to his forehead closing his eyes. Why had he waited until the last minute to write this paper? Mrs. Vaughn would be furious with him if he showed up tomorrow without it. Opening his eyes, he sighed, and glanced around the library. He unconsciously tapped his pencil and sighed again until he was jolted by a "shh" coming from the other side of the table.

ON-THE-SCENE REPORTER

Focus

This lesson focuses on conflict as an element of plot.

Grade Levels: 4–8

Purpose

Young writers need to recognize the importance of conflict when developing a plot for their stories or when reading a chapter book. Characters have problems with themselves, with others, and with the world around them. Without a compelling problem, stories would have no interest for the reader. I tell my writers to create a strong main character and then decide what problems the character needs to resolve.

I use this lesson as an introduction to the element of *conflict* in a story. Familiar folk and fairy tale picture books are chosen because they are quick to read and the characters have conflicts that are easily recognized. Selected nursery rhymes work well also.

Benefits
- develops the understanding that conflict is essential to a plot
- builds confidence in front of an audience
- sharpens the learners' ability to ask questions and follow-up questions

Materials Needed

I use a variety of picture books that are quick and easy to read. Some appropriate folk or fairy tales might be the following:

- *Little Red Riding Hood*
- *The Three Little Bears*
- *Three Billy Goats Gruff*
- *Jack and the Beanstalk*
- *Chicken Little*
- *Henny Penny*
- *Bremen Town Musicians*
- *Hansel and Gretel*
- *The City Mouse and the Country Mouse*

Examples of appropriate nursery rhymes:

- "Little Bo Peep"
- "Little Miss Muffet"
- "Old Mother Hubbard"
- "Georgie Porgie"
- "Humpty Dumpty"
- "Three Blind Mice"
- "The Queen of Hearts"
- "Tom, Tom, the Piper's Son"
- "Jack and Jill"

Description of the Activity

The students work in pairs (threesomes are also possible if more than one character is being interviewed by the reporter). I pass out one picture book or a nursery rhyme to each group. They are instructed to read the book or poem and identify the character's big problem (for example: The three pigs keep having their houses blown down by a wolf; and Little Bo Peep has lost her sheep). After the problem is identified, the groups decide on roles. One student is a news reporter and the other one is the character being interviewed. Together they work out the details of the on-the-scene interview that they will perform for the class. Reporters are reminded to use some basic reporter questions. For

Figure 4–1   The "On-the-Scene Reporter" interviews Little Red Riding Hood

example, if one or more of the pigs is being interviewed, then a reporter may ask:

- *When* did your house blow down?
- Can you describe for our viewers *what* happened?
- Did you see *who* did it?
- *Why* do you think that someone would blow your house down?
- *Where* will you go now?
- *How* do you feel about all this?

They also plan the *stand-up opening* (for example, the reporter might say, "Good evening, this is Bill Williams reporting live from the site of the demolished house of Mr. Second Little Pig."), and the *stand-up closing* (for example, "This is Bill Williams for station WXXX, reporting live from Pigsville."). See Figure 4–1. After each group finishes planning, they take turns performing the on-the-scene reports for the class.

Teacher-to-Teacher

The kids love performing these improvisations and they are frequently funny. A fake microphone can be used for the reporter and a costume piece used to suggest the book character (for example, a pig's nose for one of the Three Little Pigs).

....

STICKY SITUATIONS

Focus

The focus is on plot development (using problems to set the plot in motion).

Grade Levels: 4–8

Purpose

Characters with compelling problems are the essence of good drama. The same is true for a piece of fiction. I use this drama activity to sensitize students to the role of *problems* as a way to set the plot in motion.

Benefits
- provides an occasion for creative problem solving
- leads to a recognition that conflict motivates characters to act
- strengthens ability to work cooperatively

Materials Needed
- index cards with a "Sticky Situation" printed on each (see a list of examples at the end of this lesson)

Description of the Activity

The students assemble in the open space of the classroom. I begin with a short discussion of *plot*: "What is needed to set a plot in motion? What keeps a plot moving throughout a book?" The responses usually include the words *problems* and *conflicts* as necessary elements of a plot. I tell them that they will be working to solve some dilemmas of their own in a drama activity called "Sticky Situations."

At this point I divide the class into groups of three or four and give each group an index card with a "Sticky Situation" to solve. Depending on the situation (for example: Three kids are exploring in an attic and get locked in when no one is home), the groups need to make decisions about each character's personality and they need to resolve the problem with a logical solution. I circulate around the room while the groups plan their scenes. I ask questions, sometimes offer suggestions, and negotiate solutions when there is a dispute over character roles. After the groups have completed their planning, they take turns performing the improvisations for each other.

Teacher-to-Teacher

When planning the "Sticky Situations," I generate a list of problems based on the age and maturity level of the class. The suggestions here may or may not suit your group depending on their prior experiences.

Examples of "Sticky Situations"

- The electricity goes out in the middle of a birthday party.
- Three kids exploring an attic get locked in and no one is at home.
- After eating a meal at a restaurant, Mom (Dad) discovers that she forgot her wallet.
- Two children who are grounded for misbehavior are caught sneaking out of the house to play.
- Two students are sent to the principal's office for fighting in class.
- A child has invited her friends for a sleepover but hasn't told her parents yet.
- Two siblings get separated from their parents at an amusement park.
- A family is camping and they hear growling noises outside their tent.
- A teen comes home after curfew and the parents are waiting up.
- A child comes home with a bad report card and needs to show it to the parents.
- A child is invited to a friend's house for dinner and the mother serves food he or she hates.
- Two siblings break a valuable vase in their house shortly before the parents return from shopping.
- A child sneaks a stray cat into her bedroom when her parents are not looking. One parent is allergic to cats.
- Two students are accused of pulling the fire alarm when they really didn't do it.
- A brother steals his sister's diary and is caught by a parent.

....

TABLEAUX (LIVING PICTURES)

Focus

The focus is on the structure of a plot.

Grade Levels: 3–6

Purpose

By teaching kids about plot structure, we equip them with the necessary tools to create their own plots. I use picture books for this lesson because they are quick to read and provide clear models of a simple plot structure.

Benefits

- promotes an understanding of how plots are structured
- enhances the students' ability to visualize characters in action
- presents an occasion to communicate a plot event through a still picture
- improves the students' ability to work with concentration and cooperation
- strengthens confidence in front of a group

Materials Needed

- a well-written picture book with dramatic action and a clear conflict (example: *The Three Little Wolves and the Big Bad Pig*)
- chart paper and markers

Description of the Activity

I gather the students on the rug for a read-aloud (for example, *The Three Little Wolves and the Big Bad Pig* by Eugene Trivizas, illustrated by Helen Oxenbury). I give them a listening purpose: "Listen carefully to the story, noticing what event starts the story and the other important events throughout the plot." After completing the book, I go back to the listening purpose. As students respond to my questions, I record the answers on the chart paper creating a plot outline. There are many ways to show a plot outline, but in this lesson I draw a mountainlike structure. The beginning of the story is at the bottom of the mountain. The plot events are listed going up the mountain as the action rises to the climax and then falls as the problems are solved in the denouement. Afterwards, I tell the students that we are going to re-create the major events in the plot by making living pictures or tableaux.

To help students understand the idea of tableaux, I show them an illustration from the book. I pick one that shows the characters involved in action. I ask a group of students to position themselves to create a silent frozen picture of the illustration. I point out that they need to use their faces and bodies to convey the action and emotion evident in the illustration.

For this part of the lesson, I divide the students into groups. The number of students in each group depends on the characters in the book you've chosen. If there are five groups, I might assign two plot events to each group. The groups plan their tableaux, working to re-create the plot events in a dynamic image. While groups are planning, I tell them to consider the feeling and action they want to convey. I have a conference with each group during the planning stages. I emphasize the importance of concentration. For students who struggle with this, I suggest that they pick a spot on the wall as a focus point while they concentrate on the character's feelings. When the groups finish planning, they take turns performing the tableaux in the sequence that we listed on the plot outline. The students take their places in the performance space and I cue them with the word "Curtain!" They strike their pose and after awhile I cue them with "Curtain!" again and they relax their pose. The performances continue until all the actors have had an opportunity in the spotlight.

At this point we reflect on the experience. I ask questions about the plot structure: How does the plot get started? What is needed to make the plot exciting? Where does the climax occur? What happens after the climax? I ask questions about the tableaux: What might you add if you had the opportunity to reenact the tableaux? What acting skills were needed to create your tableaux?

Teacher-to-Teacher

I highly recommend this drama strategy for students who have limited experience in creative drama. Because it's a group activity and because there is no need to create dialogue, the kids feel quite confident as they perform. At the start of the school year, I routinely use this lesson for developing confidence, a sense of community, trust, and shared responsibility.

As a follow-up to this lesson, students create their own plot outlines modeled after the story in the read-aloud. In the Trivizas tale, there are three little wolves tormented by a big bad pig. I tell my writers to create a new version of the tale using the same basic plot idea, three little "some-things" tormented by a "big bad something."

··

YOU END IT

Focus

In this lesson, students experiment with the creation of a story ending.

Grade Levels: 3–8

Purpose

In literature circle I try to help my kids notice the endings of stories. I might ask questions such as: How did it end? Did the ending have a connection to the beginning? Did the ending fit the style of the story? Was the ending a surprise for the reader? Was there some foreshadowing to give hints as to the outcome of the story?

In this writing/drama activity, the writers create an ending for a story and then act it out for the class. Most of my writers come up with solutions that fit the story as they experiment with different endings. As teachers we need to raise the awareness of our writers that endings do matter, and that the ending needs to fit the style of the story.

Benefits

- examines story endings as an important part of the plot structure
- develops an understanding that the story ending needs to fit the style of the story
- strengthens listening skills
- builds cooperative problem-solving skills

Materials Needed

- pencil, paper
- folk tale, fairy tale, or any short story that is *unfamiliar* to the students

Description of the Activity

The students gather in our open space for a read-aloud. I give a listening purpose: "Listen carefully to the plot events in the story. I will stop reading before I reach the end, and you will need to create your own ending for the story." I then read the story and stop at a point just before the final climax. Following this, we have a short discussion about the plot and style of the story. Next, I divide the class into groups of three to four members (the number usually depends on how many characters are in the story). The groups are told to work together to solve the following problems:

- Find a logical ending that fits the style of the story.
- Outline the ending on paper making sure that the ending pulls all the pieces of the story together.
- Decide who will play each part.
- Plan the movement for the scene.
- Rehearse it quietly to keep your ending a surprise for the other groups.
- Be ready to present your story ending to the class.

Each group takes a turn presenting their scene. After each, I pose the questions: Did the ending work for the story? Was the audience satisfied? Were the problems of the characters solved? After all groups have had a turn, a question inevitably pops up: "How did it really end?" At that point I read the ending of the story. Often they are surprised that their endings closely resemble the actual ending.

Teacher-to-Teacher

During the scene planning, I move from group to group to facilitate the decision-making, the casting, and rehearsing. As the facilitator, I ask many questions to promote creative solutions and to keep the learners on task. Reminders are also needed to keep voices to a reasonable level.

I follow up this activity with an individual writing activity. I ask them to think about a book that we have read in literature circle (not all students will have read the same book). I challenge them to think of an alternate ending for the story (for example, in the actual ending for *The True Confessions of Charlotte Doyle*, Charlotte runs away from home). What might be an alternate ending for this story? Students then create new endings for familiar stories.

....

EXPLORING SETTING

Focus

The lesson focuses on the use of setting to shape the action in a story.

Grade Levels: 3–8

Purpose

Young writers need to develop an awareness of the importance of setting to shape the plot, set the mood, and reveal a character. This game impresses on the kids the importance of *showing* a setting (by including specific details) rather than *telling* the reader the location of the story.

Benefits
- develops the understanding that setting can be used as a device to reveal a character and shape the action
- provides experience in using detail to create a setting

Materials Needed

I create index cards with a different setting printed on each one. Some examples might be the following:

- a forest with thick underbrush
- a crowded cafeteria
- a hot school bus
- a gymnasium during a game
- a bus stop on a rainy morning
- an ice skating rink
- near a lake on a spring day
- the beach on a hot summer's day
- a busy city street
- a library
- a movie theatre
- outside during a snowstorm
- outside during a windstorm
- the bus stop in zero-degree weather

- the kitchen at dinnertime
- a restaurant
- the top of a mountain
- the waiting room at the dentist's office
- a museum
- a supermarket
- a clothing store
- inside a bakery

Description of the Activity

I gather the kids in the open area of the classroom and lead off the lesson with a discussion of the meaning of setting. I pick one that is familiar, such as *the classroom*. I ask the kids, "What is in this setting that establishes it as *the classroom*?" The response is usually the following: desks, blackboard, tables, kids reading, a teacher standing, and so forth. Then I ask for volunteers to come up and show the audience that they are in a classroom. I give them a few minutes to determine roles and set up the stage area. I tell them, "Your goal is to *show* us where you are by using the objects in the environment, feeling the mood, and experiencing the space around you." When they finish, I ask the audience to tell me how the actors *showed* the setting.

The kids are now ready to *explore a setting*. I divide them into groups of four or five members and tell each group to select a setting card from the stack (cards are face down). Group members go off to plan their scene. I repeat the goal mentioned earlier to the groups. After five minutes or so, each group performs for the class. The scenes are short and usually have some dialogue (caution students not to mention the setting as they talk). I often coach from the sidelines if the actors are having difficulty making the setting look real. If the setting is a movie theatre, I might coach with the following: "Show me that it's dark in there. Show me the long rows of seats." The audience's task is to identify the setting from the way the actors move and experience the place.

Teacher-to-Teacher

For students with little experience in drama activities, the side-coaching by the teacher is an important practice. It encourages the kids to creatively solve problems on the spot.

....

MOOD STORY

Focus

The lesson focuses on how writers develop mood or atmosphere in stories.

Grade Levels: 5–8

Purpose

When we examine a piece of writing in a writer's mini-lesson, I might ask my students, "What's the mood here? What's the general feeling of the piece?" They can usually identify it. "Spooky," "mysterious," "serious," and "funny" might be some responses. They are less sure of the answer when I ask them, "How did the writer create the mood?" It's important for them to know that writers create mood through *descriptive detail*, particularly settings, and through dialogue and action. We spend time in a few craft lessons looking at examples and identifying the descriptive language used to create the mood.

Once I feel that my kids understand the technique, it's time for some practice. In the following activity, nursery rhymes (other poems work well also) are the inspiration to create stories with a mood.

Benefits

- examines mood as a literary device
- develops an understanding of how writers create mood or atmosphere
- provides practice using mood as a plot device in a cooperative writing venture

Materials Needed

- copies of selected nursery rhymes
- a "Mood Story" for use as a model
- stools for a Readers Theatre (optional)

Description of the Activity

To help the learners understand the writing activity, I show a model of a completed story (see the Teacher-to-Teacher section) during a mini-lesson. Though my questions, the kids determine the mood of the piece and identify the descriptive detail that helped create the mood. Following this, I partner the students and give them copies of selected nursery rhymes. I instruct them to pick a nursery rhyme and use the main idea in the rhyme to create a story that has a specific mood. Their assignment is as follows:

- Select a nursery rhyme.
- Find the main idea of the rhyme.
- Decide on the mood that you will create (suspenseful, humorous, mysterious, sad, violent, peaceful, etc.).
- Work with your partner to write the story.
- Be ready to share your story in a Readers Theatre style of presentation.

Teacher-to-Teacher

I carefully select the nursery rhymes that I use for a writing prompt. I pick ones that have an evident conflict. Here are some examples that have worked well with my writers:

- "Little Bo Peep"
- "Three Blind Mice"
- "Little Miss Muffet"
- "Humpty Dumpty"
- "Old Mother Hubbard"
- "Jack and Jill"
- "Sing a Song of Sixpence"
- "Tom, Tom, the Piper's Son"
- "Dapple-Gray"
- "Queen of Hearts"
- "Old King Cole"

Using a model to convey the idea of mood to the learners works well. After seeing and hearing the mood story, they are ready to create their own. The following example was inspired by the nursery rhyme "Mary Had a Little Lamb."

Model for the Lesson "Mood Story"

A crash of thunder woke up Mary. She groaned as she thought of walking to school in the cold November rain. She turned on her side and scooted further down in the bed, pulling the covers up over her head. A few more minutes in my cozy warm bed, she thought, won't hurt. If I run to school I'll still be there on time. The next clap of thunder was so loud that Mary bolted upright, frightened. She sighed, pushed away the covers, and jumped down to the cold floor. Quickly she dressed and hurried down the stairs. As she passed though the kitchen, she scooped her books off the table and ran out the door, grabbing her rain cape from the peg.

On an impulse, she decided to take the shortcut through the forest. Why, she'd even get there early. Wouldn't the teacher be surprised! She jogged along the narrow path, now thick with mud after raining all night. The wind howled through the trees and the big limbs groaned as they rubbed against each other. It's dark in here, sighed Mary. Maybe this wasn't such a good idea.

The path worsened, forcing her to slow down. It was then that she heard a faint noise behind her. She looked back but saw nothing. She tried to pick up her pace but repeatedly stumbled over the rocks and mud. Again she heard a noise behind her. This time it was more distinct. If only she could run faster. If only she hadn't taken the shortcut. She kept on. The sound was getting closer and closer. She could now see the edge of the forest. Breathing hard, she used all her remaining strength to reach the opening.

Suddenly she saw the schoolhouse in the clearing. The teacher stood in the doorway ringing the bell. I made it, thought Mary, satisfied that for once she was on time and the teacher wouldn't be angry. Approaching the door, she noticed a stormy expression on the teacher's face. At the same moment, there was a loud "b-a-a-a-a-h" behind her. "Mary, why did you bring your lamb to school?" the teacher scolded. "You know it's against the rules."

THEME SCENE

Focus

This lesson highlights the recognition of theme in a story.

Grade Levels: 3–5

Purpose

In a play, as well as in a novel, themes are presented indirectly through action and dialogue. For many children, gaining insight into a theme can be challenging. Questions posed by the teacher to guide the learners' thinking are usually helpful. In this lesson, I combine a literary discussion after a read-aloud with a scene improvisation to lead my students toward an understanding of theme as an element of story.

Benefits

- promotes an understanding of *theme* as a story element
- builds group cooperation
- strengthens listening skills
- encourages a creative response to story comprehension

Materials Needed

- a picture book with a strong theme and high interest level to suit your age group (example used in this lesson: *Crow Boy* by Taro Yashima)

Description of the Activity

I gather students in a comfortable spot for a read-aloud. I explain to the listeners that they will be hearing a story that takes place in a familiar setting, a school. I give a listening purpose: "While you are listening, pay attention to how the main character, Chibi, behaves at school; also notice how his classmates behave toward him." I then read the story of a small, shy Japanese boy who has no friends because he is different from his classmates. Because of these differences, he is ignored for six years until one day a special talent is revealed and he earns their respect and friendship.

The discussion that follows is an important step that leads into the dramatization. Here are a few examples of questions that promote an understanding of the theme:

- What was Chibi's problem?
- What made Chibi different from the other students?
- How did Chibi behave in school?
- Why do you think he behaved in this way?
- How did his classmates behave toward him?
- Why do you think they treated him in this way?
- Why did the students' opinion of Chibi change in the end?

Discussion of this book is usually lively. Children can easily identify with Chibi. Unfortunately, in schools everywhere, children are sometimes ridiculed because they are different in some way: their manner of speech, the way they dress, their looks, their behavior, and so on. Students want to share their own experiences with this problem of feeling like an outsider.

After the discussion of the book, we plan an improvised scene based on the book's theme (not accepting others because they are different).

The scene is not a reenactment of the story. Instead, we use the theme as the problem or conflict and create our own situation. To do this, I use chart paper to outline the *Who*, the *Where*, and the *What*. A starting point might be a question about the setting, "*Where* will our scene take place? Will it be in a classroom, the schoolyard, the cafeteria?" The students decide that the scene will be in the classroom.

Next I ask, "*Who* are the characters in the scene?" Kids and a teacher is the response. "Yes, but each student is a specific character. Who might they be?" Gradually specific characters emerge: a child who is different named Jie, a teacher who is "nice," several class bullies, the followers of the bully, some "nice" students, and so forth.

Finally, we arrive at the most important question, "*What* happens in the classroom? Remember, every story drama needs a beginning, middle, a climax, and an end." We plan how the scene will unfold. I record the major actions during the interactive discussion. The scenario looked something like this:

- A math lesson is being taught and most children answer questions correctly.

- Jie is called up to the board and when he moves to the front of the room, there are whispers and giggles. When he fails to do the math problem correctly, there are more comments.

- At snack time, he sits alone. Students make fun of his snack as they stand around in cliques.

- When Jie goes to throw his snack paper in the wastebasket, one of the bullies trips him and he falls. Everyone laughs.

- The teacher intervenes and she is led to believe that it was Jie who was fooling around.

- Finally, one student quietly tells the teacher what happened. The bullies lose their recess as punishment.

When we *play the scene* for the first time, I interject questions that help the students think about ways to reveal their characters and the conflict to the audience. In this scene I might be in role as the teacher in Jie's classroom, but at times, I step out of character to ask questions that advance the action. During the *reflection* afterwards, I ask more questions specific to the performance:

- Were the classroom activities believable?

- What other activities could we add to establish the setting and characters more clearly?

- Are there actions that the audience sees and the teacher doesn't?

- Was the theme evident?
- What else does the audience need to know about Jie?
- Was the ending believable?
- What changes need to be made before we replay the scene?

After the reflection, the scene might be *replayed* to add the revisions that were suggested during the discussion. In the replay, students work to strengthen the central idea of the improvisation. Individuals work to build their characters and project an emotion. Students become more aware of the action in the scene and listen to each other rather than try to be the center of attention.

Teacher-to-Teacher

This lesson eats up quite a lot of class time (about an hour), but it is a valuable experience and worth the time spent working through the stages that I've described. Large group scenes are sometimes hard to manage. I frequently use the "freeze" word to stop the action while I interject a question or manage a problem. An alternative to a scene played with the entire class is to have small groups each plan a scene with the theme described in the book.

This same lesson can be used with novels in literature study. After the novel is completed, I follow up with a discussion of theme and the scene work. A short novel with a similar theme that is appropriate for intermediate grades is *The Hundred Dresses* by Eleanor Estes. Wanda Petronski is the main character who experiences isolation (similar to Chibi) in her classroom.

5 Activities to Develop Oral Language and Reading Fluency

The six lessons in this chapter focus on developing oral language and reading fluency using literature as an inspiration. The performance activities take more than one teaching session to prepare, but during each session the learners are practicing a variety of language arts skills that include reading comprehension and fluency, writing for a variety of purposes, public speaking, and active listening.

In "Puppet Theatre," they practice *retelling* a story, enacting the plot, and improvising the dialogue as they experiment with their vocal range. Another lesson that uses the enactment strategy is "Enacting Scenes from Literature." In this lesson, the students work to build a scene from a story that they have read in class. They identify a *conflict in the plot* to be dramatized. Then they follow the process of brainstorming, planning, playing, revising, and replaying the scene as they prepare for a class performance.

In "Poets Theatre," the students work in groups to plan a poetry reading that focuses on a style of poetry, the narrative poem. *Oral interpretation skills* are developed as they prepare entertaining presentations. They incorporate vocal variety, gesture, and expression to enhance the readings. Experiencing poetry in an oral presentation promotes an understanding of the poem's content and motivates the learners to write their own poetry.

"Readers Theatre" and "Radio Theatre" engage the participants in the creation of *adaptations*. To do this, they take a section of a familiar text and transform it into a performance piece. They adapt the narrative and dialogue into lines for the actors and create additional lines as needed. These performances take anywhere from three to five sessions to plan, rehearse, and perform.

The final performance activity is a "Documentary Theatre." In this lesson, the students create an *original script* based on a curriculum content topic. Documentary Theatre can be on any facet of the curriculum but the main objective is the same in each subject area, that is, to convey information to the audience. The activity is time-consuming, but has many benefits for the learners. When they create an original script, they participate in research, selecting and organizing information, drafting and revising a script, rehearsing and performing. This activity combines all strands of language arts and integrates other content areas as well. The sample lesson focuses on the preparation of a social studies script on the topic of immigration.

··

PUPPET THEATRE

Focus

The focus of this lesson is on retelling a story.

Grade Levels: 3–5

Purpose

I often use puppets to dramatize stories because of their capacity to generate verbal expression. Playing a variety of roles while using puppets provides an opportunity for children to experiment with their vocal range. Puppets are also a safe activity for those children who are shy and reluctant to participate in an oral language performance. Through the puppets, shy children often say and do things that they would be too inhibited to do normally. Finally, puppet theatre provides practice in retelling a story in a dramatic way.

Benefits
- promotes an understanding of plot structure
- provides practice in retelling a story
- encourages oral improvisation
- promotes a recognition of voice and movement as a means to reveal a character
- allows for experimentation with vocal variety

Materials Needed
- sock puppets or any easily made or existing puppets
- simple versions of folk tales
- "Puppet Play" instructions (see sample following the Teacher-to-Teacher section of this lesson)
- a puppet stage (a table or desk with a cloth thrown over it, or an actual puppet stage with a curtain).

Description of the Activity

In the activity described here, my students prepared a puppet performance for a kindergarten class. In another instance, we collaborated with a kindergarten class to create a puppet theatre using both the five-year-olds and the ten-year-olds as performers. In both projects, the kids were highly motivated to retell the stories with the puppets.

Before the session begins, I choose simple folk tales for dramatizations with puppets. The stories I choose have a clear plot line and no more than four or five characters. Examples of simple tales might be: *The Little Red Hen, The Lion and the Mouse, The Boy Who Cried Wolf, Little Red Riding Hood, The City Mouse and the Country Mouse, The Three Little Pigs*, and *How the Bear Lost His Tail*.

Session 1

I divide the class into groups and assign them a story to read. After reading, they use the instructions for the "Puppet Play" to list the main plot events and organize scenes. I instruct them to pay particular attention to the dialogue as well. By the end of Session 1, each student has a part and the outline for the play is prepared. As I move from group to group, I facilitate the character choices and suggest that they might want to include a narrator, the one who introduces the play, narrates the transitions, and sometimes ends the play with a closing narration.

Session 2

We make simple puppets (sock, bag, or stick puppets are quick and easy to make). As each group completes their puppets, they use tables or desks for the puppet stages and experiment with movement and dialogue. Some groups make props that they feel are necessary (for example, a group might cut holes in construction paper to create a "net" to capture the lion in *The Lion and the Mouse*).

Session 3

Each group does a complete run-through of the puppet play (or several). At this time, I roam from group to group to conference with the performers. I ask questions and make suggestions that address storyline clarity, management problems, and so forth.

Session 4 (The Performance)

For the performance, we arrange a puppet stage in our open area of the classroom, decide the order of presentations, and organize the audience in front of the stage. I encourage improvised dialogue rather than memorized lines. Some groups add sound effects, props, and music. I check to make sure that the audience can see the puppets and help with the transitions from one group to the next.

Teacher-to-Teacher

When I select literature for a Puppet Theatre, I consider the audience as well as the performers. Usually they are young children and the stories need to be age appropriate. The story suggestions might seem young for intermediate and middle-level students, but the focus is on practicing retelling and on preparing a performance. It is helpful for students using puppets for the first time to retell stories that have simple plots and a few characters. A simple plot is easy to remember and with only a few characters, there are fewer puppets to create. When I assign a story to a group, I make sure that each group member plays either a character or a narrator. After they read the story, I pass out *instructions to create an outline*.

Sample Instructions for the Puppet Play

- Title of the Play: _____
- List all the *characters* (including the narrator) and the actors who play each part.

Example: <u>Character</u>   <u>Actor</u>

Little Red Riding Hood   Mary Jones

- List the *scenes* in the play (scenes are designated by time and place).

Example: Scene 1: Red Riding Hood's house (early in the morning)

- List all the *major actions* for the scene.

Example: Mother is baking cookies for grandmother.

Mother packs a basket and gives it to Little Red Riding Hood.

Mother warns Little Red Riding Hood about the wolf.

- Decide which parts of the story will be acted out and which parts will be narrated.

ENACTING SCENES FROM LITERATURE

Focus

The focus of the lesson is on conflict and resolution as a plot device.

Grade Levels: 3–8

Purpose

When selecting a scene to enact from a story, I ask my students to identify a dramatic moment in the plot that also has the possibility for multiple acting parts. The characters, setting, and conflict already exist in the literature so it becomes the students' challenge to interpret how the scene would look if it were brought to life.

When my readers dramatize literature, I use a process approach. I explain to them that preparing a scene is similar to developing a piece of writing. They will go through a series of stages: brainstorming, planning, the first playing of the scene, reflecting, revising, replaying, and fine-tuning it for performance. Scenes with dramatic appeal don't happen on the first try. They evolve. I act as the facilitator during the scene building process, asking questions to help students solve problems and coaching them with side comments when necessary.

Benefits

- develops an understanding of the elements of plot, character, and setting
- promotes the understanding that conflict creates suspense
- helps the learners gain insight into the motivations of the characters

Materials Needed

- Any chapter book that is grade-level appropriate can be used in this lesson. In the following example, I use *Number the Stars* by Lois Lowry.

Description of the Activity

During the brainstorm and planning stages, we gather in the drama area in front of the easel to create an outline for the improvisation. I ask *four* basic questions and record the responses on the chart paper. The following questions and responses were used for a scene in *Number the Stars*:

- *Who* are the characters in the scene? Mr. and Mrs. Johansen, Anne Marie Johansen, Ellen Rosen, and Nazi soldiers.
- *Where* does the scene take place? The Johansens' apartment in Copenhagen, Denmark, in 1943.
- *What* is the problem or conflict? Nazi soldiers are searching the Johansens' apartment to find hidden Jews.
- *How* is it resolved? The Johansens pretend that Ellen Rosen is their daughter to save her from being taken away to a concentration camp. The trick works and the soldiers leave.

Following the planning stage, we organize groups (about six or seven in each for this scene). Each group meets to plan the scene and choose parts. When giving directions, I emphasize the need for each scene to have a beginning, middle, and an end. The beginning needs to establish the setting and characters, the middle introduces the conflict, and the end resolves the conflict (at least temporarily). I move from group to group to facilitate the planning. Each group solves the problem of creating a scene in their own way and they learn from each other during the presentations. Time for planning is kept short. I feel that it's more important to do it rather than talk about doing it.

Each group performs, and as each scene ends, we discuss what worked and what could be done to make it better. I ask questions to help with the reflection: Did the audience understand the setting? Was the relationship between characters revealed to the audience? Was the conflict made clear to the viewers?

After the reflective discussion, the groups meet briefly to talk about revisions that they want to make in the scene. Shortly after, the scenes are replayed. The revised scenes are dramatically better and usually longer because of additional movement and dialogue.

Teacher-to-Teacher

Improvising a scene from literature is not limited to chapter books. Picture books work just as well. I use both in my classroom. The kids read chapter books in literature circle and I utilize picture books in my read-aloud sessions for a variety of purposes.

Chapter books have a number of possibilities for scene dramatization. Here are a few examples:

Number the Stars by Lois Lowry, Chapter 5: "Who Is the Dark-Haired One?" (enacted in this lesson)

The Upstairs Room by Joanna Reiss

Journey to America by Sonia Levitin

Snow Treasure by Marie McSwigan

Jayhawker by Patricia Beatty

Charley Skedaddle by Patricia Beatty

Lyddie by Katherine Paterson

A Family Apart by Joan Lowry Nixon

From the Mixed-Up Files of Mrs. Basil E. Frankweiler by E. L. Konigsburg

The Clock by James Lincoln Collier and Christopher Collier

POETS THEATRE

Focus

The focus is on the oral interpretation of poetry.

Grade Levels: 3–8

Purpose

Poems are more easily understood when they are read aloud. In a Poets Theatre, the performers experience the rhyme, rhythm, and imagery of the poem as they work to interpret the author's meaning. Through the reader's use of phrasing, pitch, variety in rhythm, emphasis, inflection, and pauses, the poet's intent is communicated to the audience. To do this, the performers need to spend time analyzing the poem, then finding the best way to communicate the writer's intention to the audience. When the goal of this activity is to create a Poets Theatre performance, students are motivated to engage in poetic analysis. My kids find this more exciting than a class discussion in which the words and ideas of a poem are endlessly dissected and likely ruined for the reader.

Benefits

- builds an appreciation for poetry
- improves oral interpretation skills: pronunciation, articulation, phrasing, inflection, projection, vocal variety
- increases an understanding of the genre of poetry

Materials Needed

- variety of poetry collections and photocopies of poems
- stools for the performers (optional)
- music stands for scripts (optional) or folders

Description of the Activity

Poets Theatre (like Readers Theatre) is an oral performance of a poem(s) in which the actors interpret the poem using their voices, expressions, and gestures. The actors sit on stools or stand for the reading with their scripts held in their hands or resting on a music stand.

In this lesson, small groups of students (about six) prepare and perform a Poets Theatre. If my students have already participated in "Rhyme

Time" (Chapter 3), they will be familiar with the challenges of choral reading and oral interpretation. There are many ways to organize a Poets Theatre (I've listed some possibilities at the end of the lesson) but in this example, I organize my groups according to a poetry style, the narrative poem.

Session 1 (Introduction)

In a mini-lesson, I introduce the *narrative style of poetry*. Students listen to a poem and respond to my questions that are designed to identify the characteristics of a narrative poem. I explain that we will be preparing poetry performances using narrative poetry.

Session 2 (Planning)

I organize four groups of students (about six in each group). Each group has multiple copies of narrative poems (different ones for each group). Their assignment is to *select a poem for performance* based on the consensus of the group. Once selected, they conference with me to discuss its performance possibilities.

For this lesson, each group has a different poetry packet.

- *Group 1:* Three humorous narratives by Shel Silverstein ("Sarah Cynthia Sylvia Stout Would Not Take the Garbage Out," "Peanut Butter Sandwich," "Ickle Me, Pickle Me, Tickle Me Too")

- *Group 2:* Three fantasy narratives by various authors ("The Owl and the Pussycat" by Edward Lear, "Wynken, Blynken, and Nod" by Eugene Field, "The Walrus and the Carpenter" by Lewis Carroll)

- *Group 3:* Three rhyming narratives by various authors ("Barbara Frietchie" by John Greenleaf Whittier, "The Listeners" by Walter De La Mare, "The Village Blacksmith" by Henry Wadsworth Longfellow)

- *Group 4:* Selections by Jack Prelutsky ("Rolling Harvey Down the Hill," "I Found a Four-Leaf Clover," "Sneaky Sue," "Dainty Dottie Dee," "Michael Built a Bicycle")

After the groups select their poems for performance, they prepare the script. Preparation for performance requires a series of decisions. The following list is given to each group.

- Read the poem several times and think about its meaning. Discuss it in your group. Express in words what you think the poem is about.

Figure 5–1   *Students rehearse in the hall for a Poets Theatre performance*

- Read the poem again. Look for any unfamiliar words. Look up their meanings and pronunciation.

- Give attention to punctuation. Remember a comma indicates a pause and a period indicates a stop.

- Count the number of lines or stanzas in the poem and plan how to divide the reading into parts for everyone in your group. Include the title and the author as a line for an actor(s).

- Rather than a series of assigned solos, consider creating duets, unison parts, and two groups.

- After the lines are assigned, mark the script to indicate the cues for how you will use your voice: loud or soft, fast or slow, high or low, and stops for dramatic effect. Remember it is *how* you say your line that conveys meaning and mood to your audience.

- Consider using facial expression, gesture, and focus to emphasize the meaning.

- When all parts are assigned (put names next to the part), read through the script several times.

Note: During this entire process, I rotate from group to group, conferencing with each.

Session 3 (Rehearsal)

Each group needs time to practice their reading. (See Figure 5–1.) When all four groups are rehearsing, it can get noisy. I sometimes work with one group in our drama space while the other three groups are whispering their lines in their respective corners. Each group has a turn in the drama space with me. At this time, I help them with the oral interpretation, use of gesture, facial expression, and how to perform a stage bow. One day for rehearsal is usually enough for an in-class performance. If the poems are being performed for another class or for parents, then additional rehearsal time is needed.

Session 4 (The Performance)

Before the performance, I schedule the order of the groups. We discuss the staging needs of each group (stools or no stools, etc.) and how the transition from one performance to another needs to be smooth. When everyone appears ready, we begin the performance. Some groups choose to have a narrator and others bring music to set the mood. The classroom lights are turned off during the transitions.

Teacher-to-Teacher

Each year, I'm impressed by the seriousness with which my kids approach these performances. Once they become excited about poetry, the next natural step is to write their own.

I use poetry across the curriculum to enrich units of study. I find this particularly effective in social studies. For example, I use the poetry of Langston Hughes as one of the resources to teach a unit on civil rights. Poems such as "Merry-Go-Round," "Frederick Douglass," "Dream Variation," "I Dream a World," and "Refugee in America" have suitable content. A result of the study might be a Poets Theatre focused on a historical topic.

There are many ways to organize a Poets Theatre. The example in this lesson focuses on teaching a *style of poetry*. Other possible ways to organize a Poets Theatre are the following:

- feature an author
- focus on a theme (nature, environment, animals, humor, etc.)
- develop a performance around a topic (Civil War, slavery, holocaust, etc.)

READERS THEATRE

Focus

The focus is on adapting text into a Readers Theatre script.

Grade Levels: 3–8

Purpose

After my students complete a novel in literature study, I ask them to prepare a response activity. One of their favorite response modes is the creation of a "Readers Theatre." The group members select and adapt a section of the text, transforming it into a Readers Theatre script. After
rehearsing the script, they perform it for their classmates. The performance often motivates the audience to read the novel if they haven't
done so already.

To transform the text (narrative and dialogue) into script form, the
students use many skills. The author's writing is the basic foundation for
the script, but students need to *analyze* the section that has been chosen
for its meaning, *evaluate* which parts are appropriate, *adapt* the dialogue
into lines for the actor, and *create* additional lines as needed. The adaptation process is a natural follow-up to a Readers Theatre from a published resource. From prior participation, students know how this style
of performance works. Once they have had experience creating an *adaptation* for performance, they are motivated and experienced enough to
write an *original* Readers Theatre script (see "Documentary Theatre" in
this chapter).

Benefits

- promotes an understanding of the text
- improves oral reading fluency and expression
- encourages an analysis of the characters

Materials Needed

- a novel that has been read by the group that will create the adaptation
- multiple copies of the selection chosen for adaptation
- stools for the readers (optional)
- music stands for the scripts (optional)

Description of the Activity

The adaptation of a scene from a novel into a Readers Theatre script is a process that involves selecting a chapter, adapting the narrative and dialogue into a script, rehearsing, and finally performing. The entire class can participate in the preparation of a Readers Theatre if they are all reading novels in literature groups. Each group prepares a script from the novel that they have just completed reading. If all the students in the class are reading the same novel, groups can be formed, each choosing a different chapter from the novel.

I sometimes take the time to model the idea of an adaptation. I choose a short text (for example, the fable *The Woodman's Ax* by Aesop) as a model for an adaptation. It has sufficient dialogue and narrative and we quickly turn the text into a Readers Theatre. The ideas that are modeled during this process are listed on chart paper to provide guidelines for the creation of their own scripts. The following *guidelines* were created for the Readers Theatre adaptations:

- select a chapter or a section from a chapter
- ask the teacher to reproduce the selection for all members of the group
- read the selection several times to evaluate how it can be used
- choose a narrator to introduce the Readers Theatre, establishing the place, time, and point in the plot where the performance begins (the same narrator might also bring closure to the performance)
- list the characters and decide who will read those parts and label their names in front of the part
- cross out the tag lines ("she said") for each character
- choose readers for other important narration, label the parts with the readers' names
- omit or condense long descriptions that might slow the performance
- note any sound effects
- read through the script to practice the order of the actor's lines
- rehearse for expressiveness and timing
- practice not looking down at the script all the time
- use your voice to communicate each word clearly

The entire process takes about a week. I usually allow two sessions for the kids to prepare the script, and two sessions to rehearse and bring it to performance level. On Friday, the last session, the performances are shared with the class. During the planning and rehearsal times, I conference with each group to facilitate their work by asking questions, offering suggestions, or solving casting problems that might arise.

Teacher-to-Teacher

While students are in the process of selecting passages for the adaptations, I have a conference with each group. It's important that they choose a chapter or section of a chapter that has tension or conflict. An abundance of dialogue is another characteristic that is favorable for an adaptation.

I teach this lesson after the class has experienced a Readers Theatre using a published script. With a prepared script, the focus is on the delivery of the script and it gives the students an opportunity to learn how this style of theatre is performed. Once the learners are comfortable with the performance style, then the next natural step is to create their own script by adapting the text from a chapter book, short story, or a picture book.

....

RADIO THEATRE

Focus

This lesson focuses on fluent reading and oral interpretation.

Grade Levels: 3–8

Purpose

I first began using Radio Theatre in my social studies curriculum. It was an especially effective reporting device for research topics such as the Depression of the 1930s and World War II. During this time, the radio was an important communication medium in our culture. Families gathered around the radio console to listen to news reports, music, comedy shows, and radio dramas. I noticed that my students responded enthusiastically to the experience so my thoughts wandered to how I could apply the idea to my reading curriculum.

In the social studies experience, the students researched and wrote the script for the Radio Theatre. However, in literature study, the text of the book was used and simply adapted to create the radio drama. The adaptation was less time-consuming than writing an original script from a researched topic. I thought also that the radio broadcast was an alternative for those readers who were shy about performing. In a radio drama, the performers are not seen. They are only heard. The focus is on an oral interpretation of the script and the creation of sound effects. In a radio broadcast, it's the actor's voice that creates the picture in the listener's mind, similar to storytelling.

Because the medium relies on the sound of the voice, the performers must practice the reading to become fluent. They work on phrasing and variation in rate, pitch, and emphasis. With unseen movement, gesture, and facial expression on the radio, clear speech becomes even more important. The act of articulating, projecting, and pronouncing words correctly allows the audience to better understand the story being dramatized.

Benefits

- develops fluency: phrasing, variation in rate, pitch, and emphasis
- creates a medium for an aesthetic response to literature
- provides an opportunity to practice clear speech: correct pronunciation, articulation, and projection

Materials Needed

I use any chapter book or short story that is appropriate for my readers. I look for sections in the text that involve conflict and action and have some dialogue. For example, my students used Chapter 10 ("Let Us Open the Casket") from Lowry's *Number the Stars*. It was a tense moment in the story and there were opportunities for eight character parts and sound effects. A microphone (real or fake) and a pretend console radio (made from cardboard) are optional props, but they are effective in setting the mood for the broadcast.

Description of the Activity

A Radio Theatre is a dramatized reading of a text with narration, dialogue, and sound effects. One way to get a feel for the medium of radio is to listen to old radio dramas. There are recorded collections on CDs that include some of the most popular shows from radio's golden age. It's good listening practice and students immediately understand what they need to do to prepare for the performance. By listening to a show such as "Sergeant Preston of the Yukon" and discussing it afterward, the students realize that radio images are imagined. The medium relies on the expressive voice and sound effects.

If a short story is being read, the entire story can be performed. If it is a chapter book, then a dramatic section of a chapter that the students have already read silently is selected. This lesson might take two or three reading sessions during the preparation and the performance depending on the experience and abilities of the students.

Session 1

In literature group, we discuss and select a reading for a radio drama; usually three or four pages is sufficient. We look at the possibilities for performance. We locate the dialogue and the narrative sections. I assign or let students choose a part to read. I guide the readers as they organize the reading. In the chapter "Let Us Open the Casket" from *Number the Stars,* there are eight characters. There were seven students in the group. Therefore, some students had double roles playing two characters or a character and a narrator. I remind them to drop the tag lines when a character speaks. Once the parts are determined, the readers go off to practice.

During the rehearsal the readers practice using their voices expressively. They come up with ideas for creating the sound effects. In this selection, there are about nine effects needed: the house door closing, car doors slamming, pounding on a door, heels of soldier's boots approaching, a woman gasping, a woman weeping, someone being slapped on the face, sound of soldier's boots departing, and a car's engine starting.

Session 2

If additional rehearsal time is needed, then the students practice again reading smoothly and expressively. They time the sound effects to come in at the appropriate moment in the reading. They might add a short introduction and a closing.

Session 3 (Radio Theatre Performance)

There are several ways to present a radio drama. It can be performed informally for the teacher during a literature group meeting. Sometimes I tape-record the reading so that students can hear it later or use the tape as part of a longer radio show. Presenting the reading to the entire class is another opportunity to present their work. One reading group in my class painted a large cardboard box (opened like scenery) to look like a console radio. The group sat behind the "radio" cardboard scenery to perform the Radio Theatre without being seen by the audience. Someone in the audience was given the job of "turning on" the radio. The rest of the class listened to the "broadcast" in front of "the console." When the performance was finished, I led a discussion about what they learned from the experience.

Teacher-to-Teacher

The radio drama activity can be used several times to develop fluency while reading a book. But I find it more practical to use it as a response activity at the end of a novel. I try to have all my literature study groups working on the same type of activity. That way, other groups are not disturbed by a group of students rehearsing for a Radio Theatre. It can get noisy at times, but it's productive noise. A few reminders about voice levels usually keep rehearsals manageable.

••

DOCUMENTARY THEATRE (A CURRICULUM-BASED READERS THEATRE SCRIPT)

Focus

The focus is on creating an original Readers Theatre script to convey information.

Grade Levels: 5–8

Purpose

Documentary Theatre is the name I use to describe a Readers Theatre that is written by my students based on a curriculum content topic. It could be in language arts, math, science, or social studies. The activity involves reading, writing, speaking, and listening (the language arts strands), and integrates a curriculum topic. This activity is appropriate for fifth grade and up. Reading, selecting essential facts, organizing information, drafting and revising a script, and rehearsing and performing are skills needed to put together a Documentary Theatre.

There are many reasons why this activity is successful in the classroom, but the rationale can be stated in two words—*motivation* and *retention*. Whenever the final product is a performance, my kids are motivated to work hard during the process of researching and writing. They find that writing a script for a performance is more exciting than preparing the traditional written research report. When the script is completed, the students rehearse. Rehearsal requires repetition as they practice the script over and over. The process of rehearsing and performing the script aids in the retention of the curriculum content.

Benefits

- aids in the retention of curriculum content
- motivates the learners to research and write
- helps learners select the essential information relevant to the topic
- develops research skills
- provides practice in reading, writing, speaking, and listening skills

Materials Needed

Any curriculum topic can be chosen for a Documentary Theatre. In this lesson, I focus on a social studies topic, immigration in the early 1900s.

I used paperback picture books as a resource for the research and writing of the script. They were the following:

- *Immigrant Kids* by Russell Freedman
- *If Your Name Was Changed at Ellis Island* by Ellen Levine
- *Coming to America: The Story of Immigration* by Betsy Maestro and Susannah Ryan
- *We Rode the Orphan Trains* by Andrea Warren

Description of the Activity

The preparation of a Documentary Theatre takes time, but the results are well worth it. It can take six to eight sessions of preparation during a period of about four weeks to prepare a script. The time factor depends on the length of the material chosen as a resource. A page from a textbook, or a two-page informational handout will take a lot less time (perhaps three sessions) than researching a short book. Nevertheless, the process remains the same whether the readings are short or long.

Sessions 1 and 2

During these sessions, the groups are formed (about six in each), topics are chosen, and materials are distributed. I explain the assignment to the class. Their goal is to create a script that accurately conveys information about the topic to an audience. Like storytelling, the information should be conveyed in a way that captures the interest of the listeners.

The researchers formulate questions about the topic (who, what, where, when, and why). Several students act as readers and others take notes based on the questions that were formulated. In this collaboration, students help each other *understand, select, and organize the essential ideas for the script*. By the end of these sessions, there should be a list of important facts about the topic. I have a conference with each group to ask questions and check their recorded information.

Sessions 3 and 4

During these sessions the students organize their notes, select information that they want to use, and *draft a script* based on the information they recorded. The script must have a part for everyone. As they write, they need to keep in mind that they are not listing a series of facts, but instead they are charged with telling an exciting story to the audience. The story needs an introduction and a closing.

Sessions 5 and 6

During these sessions, the writers *revise the script* after conferencing with each other and with me. They work to create clarity and smooth transitions from one idea to another. They work to inject some humor, lively expressive language, a variation in the length of the lines spoken, and variation in solo and unison readings. After the revisions are completed, the parts are assigned, and the final version of the script is photocopied. It will probably be a two- or three-page script.

Sessions 7 and 8

Rehearsal might take one or possibly two sessions. I watch the groups to determine when they are ready to perform. During rehearsal, they practice reading fluently, picking up cues, and using their voices with expression. They decide on positions for the actors (sitting, standing, etc.) and they add gestures, sound effects, mood music, and perhaps a prop or costume piece.

Final Session (The Performances)

Usually the Documentary Theatre is performed for their classmates. At times, I invite another class or parents to be part of the audience. With four groups performing, it is necessary to *schedule the order* of the performances and *practice the transition* from one group to another to facilitate the setup time for each group. I also teach the groups how to bow with a professional flair after each performance.

Teacher-to-Teacher

A Documentary Theatre is an excellent reporting device for research in any subject area. It combines research writing with performance. When my writers write for an oral performance, I find that the writing style is natural, with the voice of the writers coming through loud and clear. This is not always true when they write a traditional research report.

6 Language Arts Performance Projects

The lessons in this chapter are referred to as "performance projects" because they take several class sessions to prepare, rehearse, and perform. Unlike the lessons in Chapter 2, which are designed as readiness for learning through active participation, these lessons assume that the kids are experienced in oral language performance techniques. They have previously participated in a Readers Theatre, for example, or have enacted a scene from a piece of literature. With that experience behind them, they are ready for extended projects that require careful planning, an analysis of literature, creative writing, and rehearsal. The performance is the culminating activity and a chance to share what they have learned.

The first lesson, "A Meeting of the Historical Society," is designed to develop *interviewing* and *reporting skills*. Students conduct interviews with family members. From the results of the interview, they compose a short speech to present at a "meeting" of historians. The second lesson presents an opportunity for the learners to practice *debating skills* and *persuasive writing*. They write factual arguments to prove their points to the opposing teams. They practice the art of rebuttal and tolerance for the opinions of the opposition.

Literature is the springboard that launches the remaining performance projects in the chapter. In "The Talk Show," the students practice *character analysis*. They use a character from one of their literature books to create a portrayal for a television talk show. The main focus of the "TV News Show" is on *research skills* and *informational writing*. Based on the setting, characters, and plot of a historical fiction novel, the learners write news and sports stories, weather segments, and relevant commercials.

In "Courtroom Trial," a simplified courtroom procedure is used to stage a classroom trial based on a literary character. To prepare for the mock trial, students use *persuasive writing and speaking skills* to prosecute or defend the accused.

In the final lesson, the writers step into the shoes of another when they write a *first-person narrative* in the form of a monologue, diary, or letter.

Once written, the presenters rehearse the character portrayals for a performance of a monologue or a dramatic reading.

Performance projects are a big time commitment and may not be for everyone, but I have discovered during my years of teaching that a performance has many educational values beyond those that I've cited in language arts. Most obvious to me is the development of group cooperation and individual self-confidence. Students set aside individual differences for the sake of a common goal. Those with low self-esteem find success onstage while gaining new confidence in their offstage role of student. Concentration and self-discipline improve as they listen for cues, work to develop a character, handle props, and make transitions.

A MEETING OF THE HISTORICAL SOCIETY

Focus

This activity develops interviewing, reporting, and speaking skills.

Grade Levels: 3–8

Purpose

Children are more confident when speaking in front of an audience if they have a prop that diverts the attention from them to the object that they are holding. In this activity, I create a dramatic situation by asking the students to imagine that they are historians trying to find out about the past. They interview grandparents, great-grandparents, or other elderly members of their family about a personal object (referred to as an artifact) that is special to them. The artifacts are brought to school and the "historians" present them at a meeting with fellow "historians." The interview questions help the students write an informative speech. These personal stories are usually memorable and provide opportunities for children to share something about their family.

Benefits

- provides an opportunity to practice interview skills
- introduces the genre of speech writing (an introduction, body, and conclusion)
- develops oral language skills

Materials Needed

- an artifact for the teacher
- each student brings an artifact (examples: family photos, a war medal, old coins, an immigration card, an award, a wedding veil, a uniform, etc.)
- a small table or movable desk and classroom chairs

Description of the Activity

Session 1

I ask students to gather on the rug in our classroom open space. I pose the question, "How do historians find out about the past?" Their responses are recorded, and with additional probing questions, the list grows. Usually, the word *artifact* appears on the list. I circle it, and we discuss its meaning.

I then bring out an artifact. In this particular lesson, I used a ceramic bowl that belonged to my grandmother. In my introduction, I tell some facts about the owner and how the object came into her possession. In the body of the speech, I explain the personal meaning it had for my grandmother and what it reveals about my family's history. In my conclusion, I tell where the object is kept and what might happen to the artifact in the future.

Finally, I tell students that they will play the role of historians searching for artifacts to bring to a "Meeting of the Historical Society." We discuss what might be considered an artifact and I mention examples that children have used in the past (an immigration card, a wedding veil, an embroidered shawl, a war medal, old coins, ration coupons, etc.). A detailed instruction sheet lists sample questions that they could ask a family member. A few examples might be:

- How did the artifact come into your possession?
- What does it reveal about your family history?
- Where do you keep this object?
- Will you pass on this artifact to someone else in the family?

The instruction sheet also reminds the learners to organize their speech with *an introduction, a body,* and *a closing.* Speeches are to be kept brief, about one minute in length.

Session 2

We set up chairs in rows and put a table in front to establish the setting of a meeting hall. See Figure 6–1. The "historians" gather in the audience and the "president of the society" (the teacher) opens the meeting and

Figure 6–1 Members of the "Historical Society" show their artifacts at the meeting

states the purpose of the gathering. The "president" also introduces each student to report on his or her findings to the audience. Most students speak extemporaneously while a few refer to their written speech. The audience often asks questions after each presentation.

Teacher-to-Teacher

I set a formal tone for the meeting. We refer to each other as "Mister" or "Miss." I encourage students to add props such as a cane, briefcase, reading glasses, and so forth to set the mood. The performers appreciate "tea" (juice) and biscuits afterwards.

If you are working with middle school students, a student rather than the teacher can play the "president." Younger students, however, need the guidance that a teacher provides by asking questions and coaching during the performance.

At times, I extend the use of the objects that were presented as artifacts to create "quick improvisations" (usually one or two lines). I arrange the players to work with a partner. (See Figure 6–1.) I tell the pairs to visually choose one of the artifacts from the center of the circle. Then I tell them to take the object that was chosen and react to it in the role of a character of their choosing. I give the partners several minutes to plan and then each pair performs for the group. For example, two students pick up an old framed photo of a soldier in uniform and one student assumes the role of the mother and the other, the role of a child. The dialogue might go like this:

CHILD 1: Mom, I found this photo in the attic. Who is it?

CHILD 2: That's your great-great-grandfather. He was a soldier in World War I.

....

STAGING A DEBATE

Focus

This activity focuses on persuasive writing and speaking skills.

Grade Levels: 5–8

Purpose

Once my students have found their speaking voices, they're not afraid to use them. They love to argue a point while debating a particular issue. Debates are an exciting medium for the kids to practice their *research skills* and the genre of *persuasive writing*. To prepare arguments that support or oppose an issue, it's necessary to research the topic. After researching, the debaters write persuasive arguments to prove their point to the opposing team. The participants use their public *speaking skills* to argue convincingly for their side. *Listening skills* are also in constant use to create rebuttals during the debate.

Debating is an especially effective tool for *teaching tolerance*. For this reason alone, it is a worthwhile project. Whether it's a current social issue or historical event, students see that arguments can be created for both sides and behind the words are real people with emotions and sincere beliefs. To listen, to respect, and to try to understand are the essence of tolerant behavior. Through debating, my students put into practice the meaning of this word.

Benefits

- provides practice in the genre of persuasive writing
- improves research skills
- provides an opportunity for an in-depth coverage of a content topic
- enhances listening and speaking skills
- utilizes critical thinking skills to form rebuttals

- provides an opportunity to practice summary skills when making closing statements
- promotes an understanding of the meaning of tolerance

Materials Needed

A topic for the debate needs to be determined ahead of time. If students are role-playing a historical character, name cards are helpful.

Description of the Activity

Staging a classroom debate can take many forms depending on the objectives of the lesson. In a formal debate, each side presents the case followed by rebuttals. This takes a lot of time. I prefer a more informal style (an all-class debate) that takes about three to four class sessions to research, conference, write arguments, and rehearse. In an all-class debate, one half of the class debates the other half. I act as the moderator, calling on one team, then the other team until everyone has had a turn to express a view on the topic. The following is a description of how I structure the sessions for an all-class debate.

Session 1

First, the topic is chosen. The debate might center on a topic in literature, history, the community, or a social issue. A *proposition is created*. In this example, the students debated a historical issue relating to the Boston Tea Party. The proposition was the following: British tea ships should be allowed to unload their tea in the Boston Harbor. Once the topic is determined, we discuss the facts surrounding the proposition. I pose the following questions: Who might be for the proposition? Who might be against it? What happens if the tea is unloaded? How much is the tea tax? Once it was established that the Loyalists wanted the tea unloaded and the Patriots were against unloading the tea, then it was time to choose sides. At first the majority want to defend the Patriot's position, but after studying the arguments for both sides, the students realized that an equally strong case could be made for the Loyalist's point of view.

　　After a proposition is created, I present a mini-lesson to *clarify the distinction between fact and opinion*. I want the kids to use logical arguments based on fact rather than emotional arguments. Ideally, there should be a balance of the two. During the lesson, I use examples based on the debate topic. "I can't afford expensive British tea and pay tax on top of that price," a Patriot might argue (emotional argument). "The taxes we pay on tea go to England, yet we have no representation in Parliament," might be another argument (factual).

Session 2

We start by *brainstorming a list of resources* that might be helpful to create the arguments. I outline the expectations for independent research:

- Find four arguments to support (affirmative side) or oppose (negative side) the proposition.

- Create a character identity for yourself.

- Write an opening in which you state your name and present your point of view to the opposing team.

- Be ready to defend your arguments with facts.

The students research while I work the room conferencing with those who may have difficulty locating information or writing arguments.

Session 3

To start this session, I present the *rules for engaging in a debate*. I explain that I will be serving as the moderator to help move the debate along, clarify a point if necessary, make sure everyone has a turn, and generally keep order if the arguments become heated. I discuss a few simple rules:

- Only a student who is recognized by the moderator has the right to speak. Everyone else needs to listen.

- Attack the opponent's argument, not the person. Be polite.

- Address your opponent by the character's name (Mr. Hancock, for example).

- Listen critically to sort out the important points made by the opponents and be ready to make a rebuttal to attack weak arguments.

- Be ready to defend your case from attack by the opposition with more evidence in addition to the original points.

- Speak clearly, using simple, direct language; avoid slang ("you guys," for example).

At this point, the students work in their groups to finish preparations. I meet with the groups and help them rehearse. I act as an opposition team member, and they try out their arguments on me. Suggestions and revisions might be made during this session.

Session 4

On the day of the debate, the teams set up chairs on either side of the classroom, the affirmative (Loyalists) on one side and the negative (Patriots) on the other. They put on name tags to identify the characters that they are portraying. When everyone is seated, the moderator begins the debate. I welcome them, state the proposition, remind the debaters of the rules, and recognize a student from the affirmative side who makes an opening statement. After the affirmative makes the first point, I call on a debater from the opposing team, and it continues until everyone has a turn.

Teacher-to-Teacher

The moderator plays a key role in determining the success of the debate. I often restate or reword an argument made by a speaker. This practice helps to clarify the point being made. It also helps those who may not be good listeners. As the moderator, I encourage the reluctant speakers by asking a leading question. This helps shy students get on their feet to state their arguments.

....

THE TALK SHOW

Focus

This lesson enhances the learners' character analysis skills.

Grade Levels: 4–8

Purpose

A "Talk Show" is an effective way for students to delve further into character analysis. In my literature study groups, the learners participate in projects after completing the book. Taking on the role of a character inspires the kids to investigate a character further as they prepare their impersonation. The format itself is easy to stage and most students seem familiar with this type of television show.

Benefits

- promotes an understanding of physical attributes (walk, posture, gesture, and bodily attitudes) as one way to reveal a character to the reader

- introduces the idea that vocal quality can define the emotions of a character, create a mood, and reveal something about the character (for example, slowness in speech delivery might create the impression of laziness or old age)

- motivates students to research a character's personality to create an accurate portrayal during the talk show

- improves listening skills
- provides an opportunity to improvise responses to questions

Materials Needed

- a copy of the "Character Analysis Worksheet" for each student (an example is included in the Teacher-to-Teacher section of this lesson)
- a table (desk) for the Talk Show host
- chairs for the guests
- simple costume pieces or props to suggest a character (examples: hats, jackets, shawls, a cane, a map, a book, etc.)

Description of the Activity

Session 1

During the first session we meet to discuss the project and outline what needs to be done to prepare for the Talk Show:

- Students choose a character to portray, selecting one from their current literature study book.
- I outline the duties of the show's host, and a host is chosen from volunteers.
- I distribute the "Character Analysis Worksheet" (see the Teacher-to-Teacher section at the end of the lesson).
- I set up individual conferences with the host(s) to formulate the talk show questions.

Session 2

I schedule individual conferences to discuss the questions on the "Character Analysis Worksheet." I try to determine if the student understands the character and we discuss possible ways to reveal character traits in the portrayal. I ask questions such as:

- How can you show what you are (e.g., a well-educated gentleman)?
- What prop or costume piece could you use to help define your character?
- Have you practiced how you will walk?
- What gestures might be typical of your character?
- What do you think is the most important information to reveal about your background to the audience?

I meet again with the host(s) to discuss the questions that each guest will be asked. Questions need to be open-ended, starting with such phrases as:

- Tell us about your . . .
- How did you feel when . . . ?
- Why did you . . . ?
- When did you . . . ?
- What did you think of . . . ?

The host also prepares several lines as an introduction for each guest on the show. The following is an example from the group that chose *Carry On, Mr. Bowditch*:

Host: I'd like to introduce Captain Nathaniel Bowditch, the navigator, and author of the famous book on navigation, *The New American Practical Navigator*. Let's all welcome Captain Bowditch!

Session 3 (Run-through)

During this time, the students create the set for the Talk Show. They decide on a name for the show and create a visual for display on the set. A run-through that establishes how the show will open, the order of the guests, and how the show will close is needed. Because the *talk is spontaneous*, it's not necessary to practice what each character will say on the show. Guests listen and respond to the questions of the host. After all guests have been introduced, they interact with the other book characters prompted by the host's questions.

Session 4 (Performance)

I often videotape performance projects. Knowing that the camera is on creates a more energetic and purposeful performance by the kids. The host opens the show with a few words disclosing the lineup of the guests for the show. The host introduces the first guest who enters in character and responds to the questions posed by the host. This procedure is repeated until all guests are seated onstage (a maximum of five guests keeps the show from lasting too long). The host then asks questions to provoke interaction among the guests. Finally, the host brings the show to a close with a few words (for example: "We've run out of time, but I hope you'll join us next week when our guests will be . . .").

Teacher-to-Teacher

It's helpful to the kids if I discuss the issue of how our English language has become more informal than it was in the past. If students are reading a book that is set in the 1800s, they need to be vigilant about modern expressions creeping into the Talk Show even though the show is itself a modern invention. Words such as *you guys, stuff, like, you know, okay, yeah* and so forth break the illusion of a character from another period.

The host of the Talk Show is key to its success. I try to lead the group into choosing someone who exhibits confidence, verbal agility, spontaneity, and energy. Another solution is to have cohosts who share the responsibility. If one is at loss for words, the other host takes over.

For this activity, the students like to use props and a suggestion of costume. The act of wearing or using something relating to a character during a performance and rehearsal helps the actor *become* the character and feel the part.

Including commercials in the Talk Show allows more children to participate. Students write and perform the advertisements. I encourage them to choose products or services that would be available in that time period. For example, the group that read *Carry On, Mr. Bowditch* had commercials for a ship's chandlery, a shoemaker, and a silversmith.

The following *Character Analysis Worksheet* is a sample of the one that I use in my class.

TV NEWS SHOW

Focus

The main focus of this extended project is the development of informational writing and research skills.

Grade Levels: 5–8

Purpose

Intermediate and middle grade students are very familiar with the medium of television. They understand the job of the anchor. They can imitate an on-the-scene reporter doing an interview, and mimic the weather and sports segments as well. They have been brought up on television and feel comfortable using the medium as a means of communication.

I use this extended project as a unique research reporting device, a literature group project, or a combination of both. It can take eight or more classroom sessions to prepare a TV News Show, but it is time well spent. The learners incorporate reading, writing, speaking, and listening skills as they prepare a script for the show. The performance project is the result of planning, teamwork, research, purposeful writing, rehearsal, and technical coordination.

Character Analysis Worksheet

Name _____ Date _____

Book Title _____

Character's Name _____

Character's Background (age, relationship to other characters, situation in the book, living and economic circumstances, education, etc.)

_____

_____

_____

_____

_____

Emotional Traits (for example: happy, confident, shy, aggressive, mean, controlling, cowardly, generous, etc.). List several of your character's traits below along with a plot action that gives evidence of that trait.

_____

_____

_____

_____

_____

Physical Traits (walk, gestures, energy level, voice, manner of speaking)

_____

_____

_____

_____

Props or Costume Pieces (List any suggestions that might enhance your character portrayal.)

_____

_____

What does you character want? What is your character willing to do to get it?

_____

_____

_____

What does your character think of other characters from the book?

_____

_____

_____

_____

Getting kids excited about research writing can be difficult, but if the reporting device is a television show, then they are motivated to do the preparation. I've noticed also that the writer's voice in a television script is more natural than in a narrative report. Characteristically, the text of the script is concise when the purpose is for a broadcast.

This type of performance project also presents an opportunity to integrate many subject areas: literature study, informational writing, and historical research. The books are read during the reading period, the research can be accomplished during the social studies time, and the scripts are written during the writing workshop along with the writer's individual conferences. In a team teaching situation, a common rehearsal and performance time needs to be scheduled during one of the periods. Integrating subjects in a project such as this provides an authentic learning situation and it sometimes is the only way to find the time to teach what is expected for the grade level.

Benefits

- presents an opportunity to practice clear speech
- strengthens informational writing skills
- improves research skills
- provides an occasion for content learning

Materials Needed

- small table where the news anchors sit
- easel or wall chart for the weather presentation
- fake or real microphone as a prop for the on-the-scene reporter
- varied props as needed for the commercials
- video camera, camcorder, or digital video (optional)

Description of the Activity

The performance project described here is an integrated literature and social studies project. My students read novels with historical settings during World War II. These novels were *Endless Steppe*, *Snow Treasure*, and *Journey to America*. After the novels were completed, the planning started for the television news shows. There are many approaches to accomplish the planning, organizing, writing, rehearsing, and performing of a project like this, but here are the steps that we took to create a television newscast.

- We *watch a news show* to become acquainted with the format and content. We list possible segments to include in the production. There are anchors who read the world news, national news, local news; on-the-scene reporters; interviews; weather; sports and entertainment news; and commercials.

- I explain to the students that the historical information revealed in the novels and the setting (time and place) determine the content of the show. After choosing a broadcast date, they *research* that time in history to determine what would have been newsworthy on that date. We brainstorm a list of resources that could be helpful in their research: history books, time-line book, Internet sources, historical maps, primary documents, encyclopedias, and so forth.

- The groups meets to decide not only a *broadcast date* for the news show, but the title of the show and *a role for each group member*. In this instance, each news group has a different broadcast date determined by the setting of the novel. The *Endless Steppe* group, for example, creates SSN (Siberian Steppe News) broadcasting in November of 1942 from Rubtsovsk, Soviet Union. World and national news items are found in history books and other resources. For example, the Russian reporters open with a story of a major counterattack by the Red Army. Local news items reflect the events in the novel. The same group reports of a speech contest at the local school. The *Journey to America* group broadcasts from Zurich, Switzerland, on November 12, 1938. For the Swiss reporters, *Kristallnacht* is the feature story. The *Snow Treasure* group (set in Norway in 1940) headlines with the German invasion of Copenhagen.

- I suggest to the groups that they *reexamine the novels* they read to learn more about the country's culture and climate. Knowing this information will help them determine the content of the weather and sports segments, and also the commercials. In the Swiss group, the commercials are for cheese, chocolate, a pawnshop, and a ski resort. The Norwegian group's weather segment includes a marine weather forecast for the fjords, and skiing and ice-skating conditions.

- During the *prewriting stage*, I conference with each group to help with a fair distribution of assignments and research. I suggest that each group member be responsible for researching and writing at least one news story. After that, they select other assignments. Several students write commercials, one works on sports, one student prepares the weather, and one student plans an on-the-scene report. The news anchors organize the news stories and plan the interviews (if any).

- During the *scriptwriting*, I remind students that pieces need to be short and clear to the listener. The *who, where, what, when,* and *why* are the questions that need to be answered in the news piece. I conference with the writers to ask about the story's lead, quoting sources, and types of questions to pose during an interview. After testing the completed material aloud, *revisions* are made.

- When the scripts are written, the groups spend time planning the show's sequence and transitions from the newsroom to another reporter or a commercial break. They sometimes try to include too many short pieces, which makes the show's rhythm choppy. A *complete run-through* before taping solves some of the transitional problems. During these rehearsals, they gather or create any visuals that are needed (a weather chart, for example).

- When the projects are ready, *the performances are scheduled*. All groups perform during the same period or I might schedule them separately. Each news show is about ten minutes of airtime. The transitions make them seem longer. I set up the camcorder and tape the news shows. The minute the countdown to airtime is complete, the students are transformed. Suddenly energy, enthusiasm, concentration, cooperation, and professionalism emerge in their performance. Knowing they are being taped sharpens their delivery. See Figure 6–2.

- When we view the newscasts, it is evident the students gained a better understanding of the literature, the history, the medium of broadcast writing and speech, and the complexities of a television news production. The performance involves them all in critical thinking and decision-making as they write and coordinate the show's content.

Teacher-to-Teacher

Writing commercials seems to be the most popular part of preparing a TV news show. Everyone wants to be involved in the fun of creating a commercial. Consequently, writing the news stories can be neglected. Therefore, it's important to make clear the expectations for the assignment. I usually ask every student to first write at least one news story. After that, they choose their second assignment from the segments of sports, weather, an interview, or a commercial.

Figure 6–2   Coanchors of the "TV News Show" read the headlines

COURTROOM TRIAL

Focus

In this activity, the students use persuasive writing and speaking skills to create an informal courtroom trial based on the situation of a literary character.

Grade Levels: 5–8

Purpose

Students in middle and secondary school sometimes compete in mock trials. These events sponsored by local bar associations have formal rules and take about four weeks of preparation. The activity described here is less formal. It uses simplified courtroom procedures to stage a classroom trial based on a literary character. It effectively synthesizes all the language arts components of reading, writing, speaking, and listening as students prepare and perform in a mock trial.

During preparation, students use critical thinking and persuasive writing skills to prosecute or defend the accused. Speaking and question-ing skills are practiced during the staging of the trial. Learners are engaged in active listening throughout the experience. The participants gain an appreciation of the difficulties that confront judges, lawyers, and jurors who are trying to resolve a case with justice for all.

Benefits

- develops questioning techniques
- provides an opportunity to practice persuasive writing skills
- strengthens public speaking skills
- enhances listening skills
- provides an occasion to practice teamwork
- expands the students' understanding of the justice system

Materials Needed

- chapter book at the appropriate reading level
- gavel, tables for the lawyers, chair for the witness box, bench for the judge, chairs for the jurors, a "Bible" prop for the bailiff to swear in the witnesses
- published mock trial script (optional); available from the American Bar Association: http://www.abanet.org/publiced

Description of the Activity

To prepare the class for a trial activity, I sometimes use a scripted mock trial as a model. Mock trials can be ordered from the American Bar Association or are available from other sources online. I have used *The Big Bad Wolf v. The Three Little Pigs*, for example, as a model of correct trial procedure. In this case, the wolf sues the pigs for attempted wolf cooking. If a scripted mock trial is not used to model courtroom procedure, then a posted list of trial procedures is helpful (see the simplified steps listed in "Session 4").

Session 1 (Introduction)

To find a case that will be tried in court, I get ideas from the chapter books that we read in our class. A few examples of cases might be:

- *Jack Arabus v. Captain Ivers* from *War Comes to Willy Freeman*
- *Captain Jaggery v. Charlotte Doyle* from *The True Confessions of Charlotte Doyle*

- *Adam Cruff v. Kit Tyler* from *The Witch of Blackbird Pond*
- *State of New York v. Mike Kelly* from *A Family Apart*
- *Sir Willoughby v. Leticia Slighcarp* from *The Wolves of Willoughby Chase*
- *United States v. Charley Quinn* from *Charley Skedaddle*
- *Colony of Massachusetts v. Tituba of Salem Village* from *The Salem Witch Trials*

Once the topic of the trial is determined (*The Witch of Blackbird Pond* is used as the example here), a lesson to introduce the students to *trial procedure* and the roles of people in the courtroom is needed. When determining roles, there are plenty of parts for the entire class: the judge, bailiff (does the swearing in), one or two lawyers for each side, a jury (usually twelve), and witnesses (any number).

Sessions 2 and 3 (Trial Preparation)

During these sessions, the teams assemble to plan the trial. One group includes the judge, jurors, and the bailiff who research the role of the judge and the jury and possibly the historical development of the jury system.

The four other groups are divided to include one lawyer in each group along with several witnesses. The witnesses need to create an identity for themselves, determine how their testimony might be useful, and help the lawyers create the arguments. The task of each lawyer is to develop arguments to defend or prosecute the case and create questions to ask the witnesses who are testifying on behalf of the defense or the prosecution.

In the example that is used here, the prosecution's task is to provide clear evidence that Kit Tyler is indeed a witch. The task of the defense is to prove that she is not a witch. Two lawyers, one from each side, also prepare a brief opening statement and a brief closing (summary) statement. It is important to keep in mind that the objective of the trial is to provide a learning experience for the students, not create a real trial. During the preparation sessions, I roam from group to group to ask questions and offer suggestions.

Session 4 (The Trial)

On the day of the trial, we rearrange the desks to look like a courtroom. The judge is in front. A chair for the witness is set to the judge's left hand. Two tables are set up for the lawyers in front of the judge and chairs are set up for the jurors on the side. The procedure (a simplified version) for the trial is as follows:

- The bailiff announces the arrival of the judge: "All rise. The Court of _____ is now in session. Honorable Judge _____ presiding."

- Both sides give opening statements. The prosecution goes first, then the defendant's attorney. They each explain what their evidence will be and what they will try to prove.

- The prosecution calls witnesses to testify, and each witness can be cross-examined by the defense.

- The defense calls witnesses to testify, and the prosecution is allowed to cross-examine.

- An attorney for each side presents a closing statement that reviews all the evidence.

- The judge explains to the jurors what they must decide during the deliberations.

- The jury deliberates, makes a decision, and the jury foreman writes the verdict on a slip of paper and hands it to the judge who reads the verdict.

Teacher-to-Teacher

This project takes time, but it is rich in authentic learning opportunities. It integrates the four strands of reading, writing, speaking, and listening while students practice literary analysis, and critical and creative thinking skills.

WRITING IN ROLE

Focus

Assuming the role of a book character, students write a first-person narrative to be performed in class.

Grade Levels: 4–8

Purpose

My kids love to use the technique of writing in role. Assuming the character of another person frees the writers from whatever preconceived notions they have about their own writing ability. When writers step into the shoes of another, they share the feelings and ideas of the characters, not their own. The writing could take the form of a monologue, diary entries, or a letter. The topics are drawn from the book's plot and the character's situation.

In addition to the experience of writing first-person narrative, this activity necessitates character analysis and comprehension of the plot to write a believable monologue, diary, or letter. Once written, the presenter rehearses to portray that person physically, intellectually, and emotionally.

As a resource for this activity, I use a chapter book that the students have completed (or nearly completed) in literature study. We discuss the characters during the group meetings, so the kids are familiar with their personality traits.

Benefits

- provides practice in the genre of first-person narrative
- strengthens literary analysis skills
- enhances reading comprehension
- allows for experimentation with solo acting
- develops speaking skills: projection, phrasing, vocal variety

Materials Needed

- chapter book at an appropriate reading level
- a costume (optional) that suggests the character (for example, a hat, a shawl, a skirt, a cane, eyeglasses, etc.)
- stools for those students performing a reading

Description of the Activity

To plan for this performance activity, it's first necessary to decide on the writing format. I like to give my kids a choice. Some students have the confidence to write and perform a monologue and others prefer reading a letter or diary entry in the role of the character. Both can be performed effectively.

Session 1

I teach a mini-lesson on the topic of first-person narrative to review the genre. I model the idea showing them a piece of writing from a previous class (from a different book) or one that I've created for teaching purposes (see the sample at the end of this lesson). We examine the writing to make a list of the characteristics of this assignment. Our list might look like this:

- Decide at what point in the book your character is speaking (beginning, middle, or the end) because characters change as the novel progresses.

- Write in the first person ("I").
- At some point in the writing, identify the name of the character.
- Reveal some of the character's personality traits through the thoughts and feelings of the writer.
- Consider the purpose of the writing. If it is a spoken monologue, the style is different than a diary or a letter.
- Reveal the setting and some plot events to the audience.
- Keep the performance to a maximum of two minutes. One typed page (double-spaced) is about two minutes of oral delivery.

Sessions 2 and 3

During these class sessions, the writers draft their pieces. They conference with me during or after the draft is completed. After the revisions are made, they type the final copy. To save time, I sometimes assign the draft for homework. During Session 2, they have conferences with their peers or with me, and then revisions begin. Final copies can also become a homework assignment.

Session 4

During this session, my kids work with a partner to rehearse their monologue or reading. The emphasis is on the oral interpretation. The actor who performs a reading needs to consider phrasing, pauses, projection, articulation, inflection, and so forth. If a monologue is being performed, then movement and gesture are added to the list. All the performers consider what costume pieces or props might help suggest their character.

Session 5 (Performance)

Usually a performance is composed of six to eight students from one literature group. There might be four students scheduled for performance readings of diaries or letters, and three students performing monologues. The following day, another literature group is scheduled to perform, and so on until all the students have the opportunity to perform their pieces.

Teacher-to-Teacher

I use the lesson "Writing in Role" across the curriculum. It works especially well in social studies. By the time my kids are creating monologues for performance, they have already experienced writing in role during a variety of lessons. They understand the genre well, but the challenge is to weave the books' characters into the writing. To do so, they practice literary analysis and critical thinking skills. Providing a model, such as the one that follows, improves their chances for success with the performance activity.

The *sample monologue model* is based on the character of Charlotte Doyle (*The True Confessions of Charlotte Doyle*) as she was at the start of the book.

My name is Charlotte Doyle and I've just come aboard this fine ship. It's called the Seahawk, one of the ships owned by my father. That's why he's allowing me, a girl of thirteen, to make the voyage on my own. Well, not completely on my own. There's Captain Jaggery. He's quite a gentleman. I hope we become great friends. Perhaps we shall take tea together. And there's the crew, but I don't expect that I'll be talking to them. Sailors are such rude fellows. They are dirty and unshaven and their clothing is utterly decrepit. I actually saw some of them without shoes. My parents would be horrified. I was horrified. But, I shall not associate with them. I shall have my own playmates when the two other families come onboard the ship. Although I think it's strange that they have not yet arrived and we're about to set sail at the morning's tide. I wonder what's keeping them.

I'm quite excited to be taking an ocean voyage all the way to Rhode Island. That's where my parents live. I'm returning from the Barrington School for Better Girls in England where I was getting an education fit for a proper young lady. Now I'm on vacation, no studies, no school to think about, and a jolly voyage ahead. Oh, I do have one chore that needs to be done every day. My father has instructed me to keep a journal of this voyage. When I arrive home, he will check the penmanship and spelling. So, I'd best go to my cabin and get my trunk unpacked and get started.

Closing Thoughts

I've successfully taught all the lessons presented in this book. But it is important to note that each year I select the lessons that I plan to use based on the abilities and talents of students in my class. Some lessons, I simply do not attempt. Others I modify based on the needs of my learners. I suggest that teachers who wish to try these lessons also make adjustments to fit their individual teaching styles, students' needs, and the classroom situation. Based on my experience teaching these language arts lessons, I try to incorporate the following practices:

- At the start of the year, I work hard to know my kids' abilities and talents. This knowledge determines my lesson selection.

- I establish a safe classroom where all learners feel free to express their ideas, knowing that they will be treated with respect. I use many of the lessons in Chapter 2 to build cooperation, confidence, and concentration.

- I try to be flexible. If I observe that a lesson is not working as planned with my kids, then I either modify it or abandon it altogether. If they are enthusiastically participating, then I might expand the lesson or return to the game or activity several more times.

- I experiment. When trying out some of the ideas in this book, the lessons did not always run smoothly the first time. But it's important to have the courage to try it, even if the lesson has rough spots. I learned from my failures. Risk-taking is part of teaching. It's also a part of being a student. I ask them to take risks when they participate in the games and activities, so I feel that I should be willing to take similar risks.

- I try to maintain an attitude of patience with my students and myself. Change takes time. If I'm presenting a new activity, project, or game, it takes a while for the students to feel comfortable with it especially if they haven't previously experienced learning through games and activities. Some students will need more time to absorb the content of a lesson than others. I try not to rush the process. If necessary, I divide the lesson into several sessions.

- I prepare my lessons carefully. When things go wrong in a teaching session, I reflect on my performance first. That's when I discover that perhaps I was unclear with my directions, or I tried to rush the process instead of using a step-by-step approach. Maybe my materials were not readily available to use when needed. It's possible that I was tired that day and my lesson lacked enthusiasm. All these factors have an impact on the success of a lesson. I try, therefore, to anticipate my students' needs with thoughtful preparation and energy.

Bibliography

Recommended Professional Reading

Booth, David, and Jonothan Neelands, eds. 1998. *Writing in Role: Classroom Projects Connecting Writing and Drama*. Hamilton, ON: Caliburn Enterprises.

Burke, Ann F., and Julie C. O'Sullivan. 2002. *Stage by Stage: A Handbook for Using Drama in the Second Language Classroom*. Portsmouth, NH: Heinemann.

Cecil, Nancy Lee, and Phyllis Lauritzen. 1994. *Literacy and the Arts for the Integrated Classroom*. White Plains, NY: Longman.

Chapman, Gerald. 1991. (Edited and developed by Lisa A. Barnett). *Teaching Young Playwrights*. Portsmouth, NH: Heinemann.

Cornett, Claudia, E. 1999. *The Arts as Meaning Makers: Integrating Literature and the Arts Throughout the Curriculum*. Upper Saddle River, NJ: Prentice Hall.

Fletcher, Ralph, and Joann Portalupi. 1998. *Craft Lessons: Teaching Writing K–8*. York, ME: Stenhouse.

Hall, Susan. 1990. *Using Picture Storybooks to Teach Literary Devices*. Phoenix, AZ: Oryx Press.

Heinig, Ruth Beall. 1988. *Creative Drama for the Classroom Teacher*. Englewood Cliffs, NJ: Prentice Hall.

Heller, Paul G. 1995. *Drama as a Way of Knowing*. York, ME: Stenhouse.

Kelner, Lenore Blank, and Rosalind M. Flynn. 2006. *A Dramatic Approach to Reading Comprehension: Strategies and Activities for Classroom Teachers*. Portsmouth, NH: Heinemann.

McCaslin, Nellie. 1996. *Creative Drama in the Classroom and Beyond*, 6th ed. White Plains, NY: Longman.

Miyata, Cathy. 2001. *Speaking Rules: Classroom Games, Exercises, and Activities for Creating Masterful Speakers, Presenters, and Storytellers*. Markham, ON: Pembroke.

Moen, Christine Boardman. 2004. *Read-Alouds and Performance Reading: A Handbook of Activities for the Middle School Classroom*. Norwood, MA: Christopher-Gordon.

Novelly, Maria C. 1985. *Theatre Games for Young Performers*. Colorado Springs, CO: Meriwether.

Rasinski, Timothy V. 2003. *The Fluent Reader*. Jefferson City, MO: Scholastic Professional Books.

Ratliff, Gerald Lee. 1999. *Introduction to Readers Theatre: A Guide to Classroom Performance*. Colorado Springs, CO: Meriwether.

Ready, Tom. 2000. *Grammar Wars: 179 Games and Improvs for Learning Language Arts*. Colorado Springs, CO: Meriwether.

Sather, Trevor. 1999. *Pros and Cons: A Debaters Handbook,* 18th ed. London, UK: Routledge.

Sloan, Glenna Davis. 1984. *The Child as Critic: Teaching Literature in Elementary and Middle Schools*. New York: Teachers College Press.

Smith, J. L., and Herring, J. D. 2001. *Dramatic Literacy: Using Drama and Literature to Teach Middle Level Content*. Portsmouth, NH: Heinemann.

Smith, Patricia G., ed. 2001. *Talking Classrooms*. Newark, DE: International Reading Association.

Spolin, Viola. 1986. *Theatre Games for the Classroom*. Chicago: Northwestern University Press.

Stewig, John Warren, and Carol Buege. 1994. *Dramatizing Literature in Whole Language Classrooms*. New York: Teachers College Press.

Swartz, Larry. 2002. *The New Dramathemes*. Markham, ON: Pembroke.

Tarlington, Carole, and Wendy Michaels. 1995. *Building Plays*. Markham, ON: Pembroke.

Walker, Pam Prince. 1993. *Bring in the Arts*. Portsmouth, NH: Heinemann.

Children's Literature Cited

Aiken, Joan. 1962. *The Wolves of Willoughby Chase*. New York: Dell Yearling.

Avi. 1990. *The True Confessions of Charlotte Doyle*. New York: Avon.

Beatty, Patricia. *Charley Skedaddle*. New York: William Morrow.

_____. 1991. *Jayhawker*. New York: Beechtree.

_____. 1992. *Who Comes with Cannons?* New York: Scholastic.

Carroll, Lewis. 1952. "The Walrus and the Carpenter." In *The Family Book of Best Loved Poems*, D. L. George, ed. New York: Doubleday.

Collier, James Lincoln, and Christopher Collier. *War Comes to Willy Freeman*. New York: Dell Yearling.

De La Mare, Walter. 1961. "The Listeners." In *Time For Poetry*, M. Arbuthnot, ed. Chicago: Scott Foresman.

Estes, Eleanor. 1972. *The Hundred Dresses*. New York: Harcourt.

Field, Eugene. 1952. "Wynken, Blynken, and Nod." In *The Family Book of Best Loved Poems*, D. L. George, ed. New York: Doubleday.

Freedman, Russell. 1980. *Immigrant Kids*. New York: Dutton.

Hautzig, Esther. 1968. *The Endless Steppe*. New York: Harper Trophy.

Hughes, Langston. 1994. " Merry-Go-Round," "Dream Variation." In *The Dreamkeeper and Other Poems*. New York: Alfred A. Knopf.

———. 1958. "Frederick Douglass," "I Dream a World," "Refugee in America." In *The Langston Hughes Reader*. New York: George Braziller.

Konigsburg, E. L. 1972. *From the Mixed-Up Files of Mrs. Basil E. Frankweiler*. New York: Aladdin.

Latham. Jean. 1955. *Carry On, Mr. Bowditch*. Boston: Houghton Mifflin.

Lear, Edward. 1961. "The Owl and the Pussycat." In *Time for Poetry*, M. Arbuthnot, ed. Chicago: Scott Foresman.

Levine, Ellen. 1993. *If Your Name Was Changed at Ellis Island*. New York: Scholastic.

Levitin, Sonia. 1970. *Journey to America*. New York: Aladdin.

Longfellow, Henry Wadsworth. 1952. "The Village Blacksmith." In *The Family Book of Best Loved Poems*, D. L. George, ed. New York: Doubleday.

Lowry, Lois. 1989. *Number the Stars*. New York: Dell Yearling.

McSwigan, Marie. 1942. *Snow Treasure*. New York: Apple Scholastic.

Nixon, Joan Lowry. 1987. *A Family Apart*. New York: Dell.

Paterson, Katherine. 1991. *Lyddie*. New York: Puffin.

Prelutsky, Jack. 1984. "I Found a Four-Leaf Clover," "Sneaky Sue," "Dainty Dottie Dee," "Michael Built a Bicycle." In *The New Kid on the Block*. New York: Greenwillow.

———. 1993. "Rolling Harvey Down the Hill." In *Rolling Harvey Down the Hill*. New York: Harper Trophy.

Reiss, Joanna. 1972. *The Upstairs Room*. New York: Harper Trophy.

Ryan, Susannah. 1996. *Coming to America: The Story of Immigration*. New York: Scholastic.

Schwartz, Alvin. 1972. *A Twister of Twists, A Tangler of Tongues*. New York: Lippincott.

Silverstein, Shel. 1974. "Sarah Cynthia Sylvia Stout Would Not Take the Garbage Out," "Peanut Butter Sandwich," "Ickle Me, Pickle Me, Tickle Me Too." In *Where the Sidewalk Ends*. New York: Harper and Row.

Speare, Elizabeth George. 1958. *The Witch of Blackbird Pond*. New York: Dell Yearling.

Warren, Andrea. 2001. *We Rode the Orphan Trains*. New York: Houghton Mifflin.

Whittier, John Greenleaf. 1952. "Barbara Frietchie." In *The Family Book of Best Loved Poems*, D. L. George, ed. New York: Doubleday.

Yashima, Taro. 1983. *Crow Boy*. New York: Puffin.

Yolen, Jane, and Heidi Elisabet Yolen Stemple. 2004. *The Salem Witch Trials: An Unsolved Mystery from History*. New York: Simon and Schuster.